DATABASES AND MOBILE COMPUTING

edited by

Daniel Barbara
Ravi Jain
Bellcore

Narayanan Krishnakumar
Fidelity Systems Co.

A Special Issue of
DISTRIBUTED AND PARALLEL DATABASES
An International Journal
Volume 4, No. 3 (1996)

KLUWER ACADEMIC PUBLISHERS
Boston / Dordrecht / London

DISTRIBUTED
AND
PARALLEL
DATABASES

Volume 4, No. 3, July 1996

Special Issue on Databases and Mobile Computing
Guest Editors: Daniel Barbara, Ravi Jain and Narayanan Krishnakumar

Distributors for North America:
Kluwer Academic Publishers
101 Philip Drive
Assinippi Park
Norwell, Massachusetts 02061 USA

Distributors for all other countries:
Kluwer Academic Publishers Group
Distribution Centre
Post Office Box 322
3300 AH Dordrecht, THE NETHERLANDS

ISBN 978-1-4419-5162-5

Library of Congress Cataloging-in-Publication Data

A C.I.P. Catalogue record for this book is available
from the Library of Congress.

Distributed and Parallel Databases 4, 203–204 (1996)

Guest Editors' Introduction

DANIEL BARBARA*   dbarbara@bellcore.com
RAVI JAIN   rjain@thumper.bellcore.com
N. KRISHNAKUMAR†   9200423@vantage.fmr.com
Bell Communications Research

There has been a tremendous surge of interest recently in mobile computing and communications. The emergence of relatively sophisticated, low-power, low-cost and portable computing platforms, coupled with the availability and exploitation of wireless spectrum, has opened exciting opportunities for making a wide variety of applications available to people on the move.

Distributed and parallel databases play two central roles in this new arena, one as essential components of the infrastructure required to support mobile users, and another as the repositories of the key applications of interest to a wide variety of users. In the first role, databases support the functions required for locating, authenticating, billing and providing administrative services to mobile users. In the second role, mobile access to databases, where the databases are fully or partially distributed across fixed and/or mobile sites, is an important emerging area, e.g., for applications such as mobile sales, personalized information services, and factory operations.

There remain interesting database challenges, however, before the requirements and constraints imposed by mobile computing can be fully met. The research community has begun addressing these issues recently at several workshops and conferences. In this Special Issue, we called for research contributions addressing issues relating to the role of distributed and parallel databases in mobile computing.

One of the novel approaches advocated in recent years for taking advantage of the broadcast nature of the wireless medium has been to periodically broadcast information required by mobile clients, thus effectively placing the "database on the air". Since individual mobile clients only want a portion of the information at any given time, several techniques have been suggested for indexing and organizing the data in the broadcast so as to reduce the time or resource consumption required by the clients to access the data. Typically mobile computers have limited resources compared to their fixed counterparts, particularly in terms of limited battery life. The paper by Lee and Lee ("Using Signature Techniques for Information Filtering in Wireless and Mobile Environments") considers the use of signature techniques for this purpose, with the objective of minimizing the power consumption by the mobile client. Their investigation suggests a multi-level signature scheme for identifying and filtering the data in the broadcast.

*Previously at Matsushita Information Technology Lab., Princeton, NJ.
†Current address: Fidelity Systems Company, Fidelity Investments, Boston, MA 02109.

A key requirement for successful research, development and deployment of effective mobile computing systems and solutions is to identify and investigate compelling, core applications which will be required by mobile users. Workflow management systems have recently attracted a lot of attention as tools for automating business processes. The paper by Alonso et al. ("Exotica/FMDC: A Workflow Management System for Mobile and Disconnected Clients") investigates the issues raised when mobile computers are to be supported by an existing workflow management system while preserving correctness of the overall system. The authors focus on the ramifications of supporting mobile clients which may voluntarily or involuntarily be disconnected from the rest of the system from time to time.

It is clear that not only will mobile computers be limited in terms of their computing resources, but will be used in situations which introduce additional constraints, e.g., typing is to be kept at a minimum, a large display screen is not feasible, etc. Examples include use by field service and medical emergency personnel. The paper by Massari et al. ("Supporting Mobile Database Access through Query by Icons") describes how a query processing facility called Query By Icon (QBI) has been extended to support mobile clients, with their limited battery power, frequent disconnection, etc. The facility allows mobile users to compose database queries with minimal or no knowledge of the database structure and location, and to do so using minimal typing.

The system engineering issues involved in supporting data access by mobile users are also of considerable importance. The paper by Liu and Maguire ("A Mobility-Aware Dynamic Database Caching Scheme for Wireless Mobile Computing and Communication") considers how the utilization of the wireless bandwidth—a precious resource in the mobile computing system—can be improved when mobile clients cache the information broadcast in a periodic wireless broadcast database. They observe that if the caches are kept up-to-date via broadcast of invalidation reports, all the reports should not be broadcast throughout the system, but those relevant to a particular client should be broadcast only where the client is currently located. The authors present a system design and a performance evaluation of the effectiveness of this idea.

We hope the papers presented in this Special Issue will stimulate further investigation in this area. The area of databases and mobile computing continues to attract growing interest. For this Special Issue we received eleven submissions, of which we were able to accept only four. We thank all the authors for their submissions. We also thank the referees for reviewed the submitted papers. We would also like to thank the Editor-in-Chief Ahmed Elmagarmid, Area Editor Amit Sheth, and the rest of the Editorial Board for the opportunity to edit this Special Issue. Finally, we thank Judith Kemp and Bob Holland of Kluwer for their assistance with this issue.

Distributed and Parallel Databases 4, 205–227 (1996)
© 1996 Kluwer Academic Publishers.

Using Signature Techniques for Information Filtering in Wireless and Mobile Environments

WANG-CHIEN LEE   wlee@cis.ohio-state.edu
Dept. of Computer and Information Science, The Ohio State University, Columbus, Ohio 43210-1277

DIK LUN LEE   dlee@cs.ust.hk
Department of Computer Science, University of Science and Technology, Clear Water Bay, Hong Kong

Received May 1, 1995; Accepted February 12, 1996

Recommended by: Daniel Barbara, Ravi Jain and Narayanan Krishnakumar

Abstract.   This paper discusses the issue of power conservation on mobile clients, e.g., palmtop, in wireless and mobile environments. It suggests that techniques using signatures are suitable for realtime information filtering on mobile clients. Three signature-based approaches, namely simple signature, integrated signature and multi-level signature schemes, are presented. The cost models for the access time and tune-in time of these three approaches are developed. We show that the multi-level signature method is in general better than the other two methods.

Keywords: indexing, information broadcast, mobile computing, personal communication

1. Introduction

Rapid advances in wireless data networks and personal computing have opened up new services to mobile users. Various commercial and experimental mobile computing and communication clients have appeared recently [5, 20]. It is envisioned that these mobile clients will be as popular as walkmans and portable TVs in the near future and promise to revolutionize the information service market. In a wireless communication environment, users with mobile clients are free to access information services and communicate with other users without geographical limitations. To meet the market needs, ubiquitous services, such as fax-oriented messengers, nomadic conferencing and computing, mail-triggered applications, and information broadcasting, will emerge as some of the most important research topics in the next decade [10].

The application of information broadcast is numerous. For example, while on the road, mobile users may receive traffic and weather information on the air [17]; investors may access current information about stocks; customers in a shopping mall may query about the stores, products, and sale information [3]. In this paper, we consider the problems with information broadcast services for users equipped with battery powered mobile clients.

We may consider two modes of operations in information broadcast applications. For mobile clients with transmit capability, they may send user queries to the central server, which collects the queries over a period of time and broadcasts the requested information on the channel. The mobile clients are responsible for identifying the information they need from the channel. For mobile clients without transmit capability, the central server will broadcast all of the information on the channel in a certain order, the mobile clients listen to the channel and select the information requested by the users. Inherently, broadcasting is unreliable in an error-prone wireless communication environment. The issues of receiving information correctly and recovering from errors are important and thus need further study. However, they are beyond the scope of this paper. In this paper, we investigate indexing techniques for filtering broadcast information on the air with the assumption that the mobile clients have no transmit capability.

1.1. Power conservation and information broadcasting

A major problem with mobile clients is their power supplies. In order to make mobile clients portable, small batteries, such as AA or AAA batteries, are likely to be used [4]. However, these batteries have small capacity and need recharging or replacement after a short period of usage. Although processors and memories consuming less power have been developed (e.g., the *Hobbit* chip from AT&T and energy efficient chip designs at Berkeley [6]), new generations of faster chips with high clock frequency will continue to demand more and more power. Therefore, power conservation is an important issue for applications in the mobile computing environment.

There are two factors affecting power consumption in mobile clients: (1) mobile clients can be switched between *active* mode (full power) and *doze* mode [9], and (2) receiving messages consumes less energy than sending messages. Methods have been proposed for energy efficient query optimization [2] and information broadcasting [11, 12].

In the wireless environment, broadcasting is an attractive method for the dissemination of information to mobile clients because base stations are equipped with powerful communication equipments but mobile clients, restricted by cost, portability and power, can afford little or no transmission capability. Moreover, broadcasting can scale up to an arbitrary number of users. In contrast to accessing traditional storage media, the performance of accessing information on air does not degrade as the number of users increases. In this paper, we consider power consumption issues of the broadcasting-based applications.

In broadcasting, the base station sends out a series of *information frames*. (See figure 1.) An information frame is a logical unit of information broadcast on the air and may consist of multimedia information, including text, image, audio/video and other related data. Frames

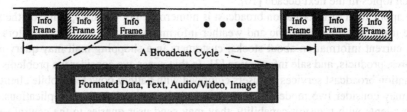

Figure 1. Information stream.

4

may vary in size; they consist of *packets* which are the physical unit of broadcasting. A frame contains a header (not shown in the figure) for synchronization as well as meta-information indicating the type and length of the frame. At the receiving end, users are allowed to specify conditions on the frames they are interested in. The mobile clients will only present to the users frames matching the conditions. Since the information frames are periodically broadcast, a complete broadcast of the information frames is called a *broadcast cycle*. From the user's viewpoint, the broadcast information is perceived as a stream of frames flowing along the time axis. Logically, there is no specific start and end frames for a broadcast cycle; a broadcast cycle starts with any frame and ends when the frame appears again. In a broadcast cycle, some important information frames may be replicated (i.e., frames with the same contents but treated as different frames). Information frames may be inserted, deleted, and modified. The updates are reflected in the subsequent broadcast cycles.

The duration that a mobile client must stay in active mode to answer a query is called the *tune-in time*, which is proportional to power consumption. *Access time* is the time required to collect all qualified frames. Without any access aid, both the tune-in time and access time are equal to the length of the broadcast cycle, because it is necessary to scan through all of the frames in a broadcast cycle to pick up the qualified frames. This is very inefficient in power consumption, because typically only a few frames in a cycle satisfy the user request.

Access methods can be developed so that the mobile client can be turned off when the frame being broadcast is not qualified. By switching between active and doze modes, power consumption is reduced. In order to tell which frames would qualify ahead of time, auxiliary information about the contents of the frames must be added. Due to the limited number of broadcast channels available, we assume that only one channel is used for both primary and auxiliary information. With only one channel, the auxiliary information will increase the length of a broadcast cycle and thus increase access time. However, it will reduce tune-in time, because it allows the mobile clients to avoid tuning into unwanted information frames. Thus, we must tradeoff between access time and tune-in time when we consider what auxiliary information is to be used and how it is going to be organized.

Two approaches, namely, hashing and indexing [11, 12], have been proposed in the literature for encoding auxiliary access information for wireless broadcasting information services. Since indexes based on one single key were assumed in these studies [11, 12], these methods won't support general queries involving various attributes of the information frame.

A major difference between indexing disk-resident data and indexing broadcast data is that disk-based indexing allows random access to data whereas data on a broadcast channel must be accessed sequentially. This property significantly changes the cost factors of indexing techniques. The focus of this paper is on the application of the signature file technique, to be described next, on indexing broadcast information. Signature file techniques are known to be slow compared to tree structures. However, in a broadcast channel, they become very attractive as tree structures lose their advantage in speed. On the other hand, the simplicity of the signature file makes it highly suitable for realtime information filtering under stringent processor speed and memory size.

5

record | IBM | Computer |

attribute	bit strings
IBM	001 000 110 010
Computer	000 010 101 001
record signature ($\lor$)	001 010 111 011

Queries	Query Signatures	Results
1) IBM	001 000 110 010	← true match
2) GE	010 001 000 011	← no match
3) Ford	001 000 111 000	← false drop

Figure 2. Signature generation and comparison.

1.2. The signature technique

Signature methods have been used extensively for text retrieval [8], image database [14], multimedia database [16, 19] and other conventional database systems [7]. A signature is basically an abstraction of the information stored in a record or a file. By examining the signature only, we can estimate whether the record contains the desired information.

A signature of a record is formed by first hashing each value in the record into a bit string and then superimposing together all bit strings generated from the record into the record signature, S_i. During filtering, a query signature, S_Q, is constructed in the same way and then compared to the record signatures. There are three possible outcomes of the comparison:

- the record matches the query; that is, for every bit set in the query signature, the corresponding bit in the record signature is also set (i.e., $S_Q \land S_i = S_Q$);
- the record doesn't match the query (i.e., $S_Q \land S_i \neq S_Q$);
- the signature comparison indicates a match but the record in fact does not match the search criteria.

We call the first case *true match* and the last case *false drop*, respectively. To eliminate false drops, the record must be compared directly with the query after the record signature signifies a match. A signature failing to match the query signature guarantees that the corresponding record can be ignored. Figure 2 depicts the signature generation and comparison processes of a company record having two attributes, name and type.

In a mobile environment, the signature technique offers the following advantages for information filtering:

- Signature techniques may be generally applied to various types of information media. This is important since the broadcast information may contain multimedia in addition to formatted data.
- Signature techniques are particular good for multi-attribute retrieval, which is necessary for specifying precise filtering conditions.

- Signatures are very easy to generate and search; thus, they are suitable for mobile clients where realtime searching with limited buffer space is required.
- A signature is very short compared to an information frame. Moreover, the length of the signature can be controlled by varying the number of values hashed into a signature (with the corresponding effect on the false drop probability).
- A signature file is basically a sequential file structure. This makes it easy to "linearize" the signature file for broadcasting on air and scanning by a mobile client, whereas a tree based access structure will lose the speed advantage because random access cannot be done on a broadcast channel.

The rest of the paper is organized as follows. In Section 2, three signature schemes for information indexing and filtering are presented; their performance is evaluated in terms of access time and tune-in time. Section 3 is a review of related work. Finally, Section 4 concludes the paper.

2. Information broadcasting using the signature technique

Signatures are constructed from the information frames and broadcast together with the information frames. The signatures may be broadcast as a group before the information frames or interleaved with the corresponding frames. Figures 3 and 4 illustrate these two approaches. The period of time from the moment a user tunes in until the first signature is received is called *the initial probe time*, while the time for the CPU to change from the doze mode to active mode, or vice versa, is called *the setup time*. Since the non-interleaved method reduces the number of switches between active and doze modes at the mobile clients, it has a smaller total setup time and simpler software at the broadcasting end than the interleaved approach. However, since the user may start monitoring the broadcast channels at any moment, missing the signature segment means the user has to wait until the next broadcast cycle to access the signatures. The non-interleaved method results in a

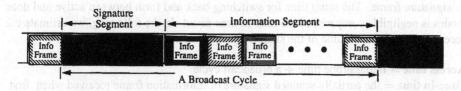

Figure 3.   Non-interleaved signatures.

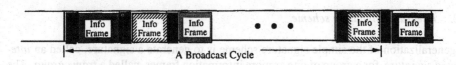

Figure 4.   Interleaved signatures.

longer initial probe time, and thus a longer access time delay, than the interleaved approach. Moreover, the setup time of a CPU for a typical mobile client, is less than 20 msec (e.g., *Piranha* chip from AT&T), and is expected to be decreasing. Compared to the time to skip an information frame, the advantage in setup time of the non-interleaved method may not justify its long delay on access time. Thus, we only consider interleaved approaches in this paper. Note that during the initial probe time, the user may choose to switch to doze mode until a signature is encountered or to remain in active mode to scan for qualified information frames without the help of signatures. The former will save energy, while the latter may return qualified information frames earlier. Since the focus of the paper is on energy saving, we will assume that the mobile client stays in doze mode during the initial probe time.

Different schemes may be used to organize signatures and information for broadcasting. In this paper, we discuss three signature methods based on interleaving.

2.1. Simple signature scheme

The most intuitive approach for interleaving signatures with information frames is to construct a signature, called *simple signature*, for each information frame. The signature frame is broadcast before the corresponding information frame (see figure 4).

When a mobile user wants to retrieve information from the broadcast channel, she/he specifies a query on a mobile client. A query signature S_Q is generated based on the specified query. Then the mobile client tunes into the channel and uses S_Q to compare with the simple signatures received. When a match is found, the corresponding information frame is received by the mobile client for further checking in order to eliminate false drops. If the frame is not a false drop, it will be retained in the result set. When the simple signature does not match with the query signature, the mobile client will fetch the frame size from the header of the information frame and switch into doze mode until the next signature frame arrives. If most of the simple signatures don't match with the query signature, the mobile client will stay in doze mode for the most part of a broadcast cycle, thus saving a lot of energy.

The average initial probe time is half of the average size of an information frame and its signature frame. The setup time for switching back and forth between active and doze modes is negligible compared to the tune-in time saved. In the following, we estimate the access time and tune-in time of the simple signature scheme.

Access time = initial probe time + a broadcast cycle.
Tune-in time = the partially scanned signature or information frame received when first tune in + every signature in a broadcast cycle + false drop and true match information frames in the cycle.

2.2. Integrated signature scheme

A generalization of the simple signature scheme is to generate a signature, called an *integrated signature*, for a group of one or more information frames, called a *frame group*. The integrated signature is broadcast before the frame group. Figure 5 shows the arrangement

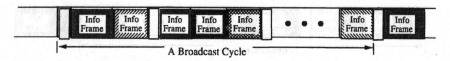

Figure 5. Integrated signature scheme.

of the signatures and frame groups. A signature may index any number of information frames. As shown in the figure, the first signature indexes two information frames while the next signature indexes three information frames. In this scheme, the header of an information frame has to provide information such as the period of time to pass by until the next signature frame arrives.

During the initial probe time, we assume the mobile client to stay in doze mode after it actively monitors the initial partial signature or information frame encountered. The mobile client will wake up upon the arrival of the next integrated signature and start filtering. The filtering procedure of the integrated scheme is similar to the simple signature scheme. When an integrated signature does not match with the query signature, the information frames it indexes can be skipped. When a signature match occurs, all of the information frames associated with the signature have to be checked for false drop elimination. Some of the information frames in the true match group may not qualified for the query, thus resulting in unnecessary power consumption.

An unmatched integrated signature allows the mobile client to stay in doze mode for a longer period of time, thus avoiding frequent switching between modes. However, squeezing more information from multiple frames into a signature will increase the probability of false drops. Therefore, we have to properly adjust the size of the signatures or reduce the number of bit strings superimposed into the integrated signatures in order to maintain the filtering capability. Grouping together similar information frames (those having the same values for most of the indexed attributes) to generate the integrated signature has the same effect as as reducing the number of bit strings superimposed. Thus, the grouping will produce more concentrated hits and reduce false drops. This method is good when the order of the information frames is not important.

In this scheme, the average initial probe time is half the average size of an frame group and its integrated signature. The following is the estimation of average initial probe time, access time and tune-in time:

Access time = initial probe time + a broadcast cycle.
Tune-in time = the partial integrated signature or information frame scanned + every integrated signature in a cycle + false drop and true match frame groups.

Note that every information frame in the true match group has to be compared with the query, even though only one qualified frame within the group may exist.

2.3. Multi-level signature scheme

The multi-level scheme is a combination of the simple signature and integrated signature schemes [13]. It consists of multiple levels of signatures. Signatures at the upper levels

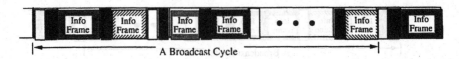

Figure 6. Multi-level signature scheme.

are integrated signatures and those at the lowest level are simple signatures. We assume that the header of an information frame provides information such as its frame size and the period of time to pass by until the next integrated signature frame arrives. Figure 6 illustrates a 2-level signature scheme. The white signatures in the figure are integrated signatures. An integrated signature indexes all of the information frames between itself and the next integrated signature of the same or at a higher level. (In the figure, an integrated signature indexes two information frames.) The black signatures are simple signatures for the corresponding information frames. The integrated and simple signatures may use different frame sizes in order to minimize the tune-in time. However, the signatures may be set to the same size to simplify the signature generation and match processes on the base station and mobile clients. To reduce the false drop probability, the hashing functions used in generating the integrated signatures and simple signatures are different.

To answer a query, a query signature is generated for each level of the signatures. Take the 2-level signatures in figure 6 as an example. Query signatures S_Q and S'_Q are constructed for the integrated and simple signature levels, respectively. After the initial probe period, if an integrated signature is received, S_Q is used to match with the signature.

1. If the match fails, the mobile client will go into doze mode until the next integrated signature arrives, i.e., skip the whole frame group.
2. If the match is successful, S'_Q is used to match with each of the simple signatures in the frame group.

   - If S'_Q and a simple signature match, the corresponding information frame is received for false drop elimination.
   - If not, the mobile client may go into doze mode until the next simple signature arrives.

On the other hand, if a simple signature is received, we pretend that the integrated signature for the current frame group has a successful match with S_Q. Thus the filtering will start with step 2 of the above procedure.

The access time and tune-in time for the multi-level scheme are as follows.

Access time = initial probe time + a broadcast cycle

Tune-in time = the partial signature or information frame scanned + all of the integrated signatures in a cycle + simple signatures associated with the qualified integrated signatures + false drop and true match information frames associated with the matched simple signatures.

2.4.   Performance analysis

There are several factors affecting the tune-in time and access time of the signature schemes. For example, we must consider the number and the size of the signatures, the false drop probability of the signatures, and the initial probe time. A performance evaluation has to take these factors into account. The false drop probability may be controlled by the size of the signatures. Note that the choice of the length of the information frame depends on the application. Based on the information frame size selected, the signature length can be chosen to yield a specific false drop probability. The initial probe time is related to the number of signatures interleaved with the information frames; the access time and tune-in time are dependent on the number, size and false drop probability of the signatures.

Frame is the logical unit of information in broadcasting, while packet is the physical unit of the broadcasting. Therefore, in our analysis, the performance is estimated in terms of packets.

In the following, we use *frame signature* to refer to the signatures of information frames, i.e., simple and integrated signature frames.

2.4.1. Symbols and parameters.

A: number of information frames in a broadcast cycle.
A_f: number of information frames received due to false drops.
A_t: number of information frames received due to true matches.
I: number of integrated signatures in a broadcast cycle.
I_f: number of integrated signatures matched as false drops.
I_t: number of integrated signatures which are true matches.
P_f: false drop probability.
P_f^s: false drop probability for simple signatures.
P_f^i: false drop probability for integrated signatures.
P_s: selectivity of a query.
k: the number of information frames indexed by an integrated signature.
l: locality of true matches (average number of true matches in a frame group).
m: length of a signature in bits.
n: the average number of packets in an information frame.
p: the number of bits in a packet.
r: the number of packets in a signature ($r = \lceil m/p \rceil$).
s: the number of bit strings which are superimposed into a signature.
w_b: number of 1's in a bit string generated from hashing one value.
w_f: average number of 1's in a frame signature.
$\bar{w}_f$:   average number of 0's in a frame signature ($\bar{w}_f = m - w_f$).

2.4.2. False drop probability.
The false drop probability is an important factor for the estimation of access time and tune-in time. The false drop probability P_f is generally defined as:

$$P_f = \frac{A_f}{A - A_t}$$

where A is the number of information frames in a broadcast cycle, A_f is the number of information frames received due to false drops, and A_t is the number of information frames received due to true matches.

To apply signature techniques to information filtering in the mobile computing environment, we have to compare the query signature with the frame signature of every information frame in order to screen out unqualified information frames. The false drop probability can be estimated assuming unsuccessful searches [8], under which a false drop occurs when each of the bits in the frame signature corresponding to the 1's in the query signature is set to 1. Let α_i and β_i be the ith bit of the query signature and a frame signature, respectively. A false drop occurs when the following condition holds:

$$\text{if } \alpha_i = 1 \quad \text{then } \beta_i = 1, \ 1 \leq i \leq m$$

or when

$$\text{if } \beta_i = 0 \quad \text{then } \alpha_i = 0, \ 1 \leq i \leq m$$

Let $\bar{w}_f$ be the average number of 0's in a frame signature, i.e., average number of bits in a frame signature set to 0. Therefore, the false drop probability is the probability for at least $\bar{w}_f$ bits in the query signature set to 0. For a query with single key value, the false drops probability is as follows.

$$P_f = \text{Probability}\big[\alpha_1 = 0 \wedge \alpha_2 = 0 \wedge \cdots \wedge \alpha_{\bar{w}_f} = 0\big]$$

where $\bar{w}_f$ is the average number of 0's in a frame signature.

In the following, we give two lemmas for the average number of 0's in a signature and the false drop probability for the signature technique. However, due to space constraint, the derivations of the lemmas are not included in the paper. Interested readers are referred to [15] for details.

Lemma 2.4.1. *Given the length of a signature in bits, m, the number of bit strings superimposed into the signature, s, and the number of 1's set in the bit strings, w_b, the average number of 0's in the signature is:*

$$\bar{w}_f \approx me^{-w_b s/m}$$

Next, we derive P_f, assuming an unsuccessful search of a single value query, for the signature technique. Multiple value queries which are Boolean combinations of single value queries may be derived in a similar way. Based on P_f, the estimation for the access time and tune-in time can be derived.

Lemma 2.4.2. *Given the length of a signature in bits, m, the number of bit strings superimposed into the signature, s, and the number of 1's set in the bit strings, w_b, the false* *drop probability for the signature is*:

$$P_f = \left(1 - \frac{\bar{w}_f}{m}\right)^{w_b}$$

where $\bar{w}_f$ *is the average number of* 0's *in the signature.*

Based on Lemmas 2.4.1 and 2.4.2, the false drop probability for a signature can be derived as follows:

$$P_f \approx (1 - e^{-w_b s/m})^{w_b}$$

The above formula is optimal when [18]:

$$w_b = w_{opt} = m \cdot \ln 2/s$$

Consequently, the optimal false drop probability is:

$$P_f \approx 0.5^{w_{opt}}$$

2.4.3. Cost models.   In this section, we develop the cost models for the initial probe time, access time and tune-in time for the three signature schemes. We use the number of packets as the unit for time estimation. To simplify our discussion, we assume that every information frame has the same number of packets. Therefore, the total number of packets for the data part is:

$$\text{DATA} = A \cdot n.$$

Simple signature scheme.   The total number of packets for the simple signatures in a cycle is:

$$\text{SIG}_s = A \cdot \lceil m/p \rceil = A \cdot r$$

We use CYCLE_s to denote the length of a complete cycle for the simple signature scheme:

$$\text{CYCLE}_s = \text{SIG}_s + \text{DATA}$$

The initial probe time is the period of time before the next signature arrives. Therefore, the average initial probe time is:

$$\text{PROBE}_s = (r + n)/2$$

After the initial probe period, the filtering process will last for a complete broadcast cycle. Therefore, the average access time is the sum of the initial probe time and the broadcast cycle.

$$ACCESS_s = PROBE_s + CYCLE_s$$
$$= (A + 0.5) \cdot (r + n)$$

Let PT_s denote the period in which the mobile client is active during the initial probe time.

$$PT_s = \frac{r \cdot 1/2 \cdot r + n \cdot 1/2 \cdot n}{r + n}$$
$$= \frac{r^2 + n^2}{2(r + n)}$$

To estimate the tune-in time, we have to first estimate the number of true matches. Let P_s denote the selectivity of a query, the number of true matches is:

$$A_t = A \cdot P_s$$

In the filtering process, the mobile client has to tune in for all of the signature frames. In addition, it has to tune in for the true match and false drop information frames as well. Therefore, the tune-in time is:

$$TUNE_s = PT_s + SIG_s + A_t \cdot n + A_f \cdot n$$
$$= PT_s + SIG_s + A_t \cdot n + P_f^s \cdot A \cdot n - P_f^s \cdot A_t \cdot n$$
$$= PT_s + SIG_s + A \cdot n \cdot P_s + A \cdot n \cdot P_f^s - A \cdot n \cdot P_s \cdot P_f^s$$
$$= PT_s + SIG_s + DATA \cdot P_s + DATA \cdot P_f^s - DATA \cdot P_s \cdot P_f^s$$

Integrated signature scheme. Assume that k information frames are grouped together in generating an integrated signature. The total number of integrated signatures is:

$$I = \lceil A/k \rceil$$

The total number of packets for the integrated signatures in a cycle is:

$$SIG_i = I \cdot r = \lceil A/k \rceil \cdot r$$

Therefore, the length of a complete broadcast cycle for the integrated signature scheme is:

$$CYCLE_i = SIG_i + DATA$$

The average initial probe time is:

$$PROBE_i = (r + k \cdot n)/2$$

Similar to the simple scheme, the access time for the integrated scheme is:

$$\text{ACCESS}_i = \text{PROBE}_i + \text{CYCLE}_i$$

Let PT_i denote the duration in which the mobile client is kept active during the initial probe time.

$$\text{PT}_i = \frac{r \cdot 1/2 \cdot r + n \cdot k \cdot 1/2 \cdot n}{r + n \cdot k}$$
$$= \frac{r^2 + n^2 \cdot k}{2(r + n \cdot k)}$$

The integrated scheme is good for broadcast with similarity among information frames, because similar information frames can be grouped together in generating the integrated signatures. Consequently, when a true match occurs, the frame group is likely to contain more than one qualified information frame. Let l denote the average number of qualified frames corresponding to a matched integrated signature. The tune-in time for the integrated signature scheme is:

$$\text{TUNE}_i = \text{PT}_i + \text{SIG}_i + I_t \cdot n \cdot k + I_f \cdot n \cdot k$$
$$= \text{PT}_i + \text{SIG}_i + \left\lceil \frac{A \cdot P_s}{l} \right\rceil \cdot n \cdot k + P_f^i \cdot I \cdot n \cdot k$$
$$\approx \text{PT}_i + \text{SIG}_i + \frac{P_s \cdot k}{l} \cdot \text{DATA} + P_f^i \cdot \text{DATA}$$

Note that P_f^i is a function of the number of bit strings superimposed, which we expect to be smaller than $s \cdot k$.

Multi-level signature scheme. In this section, we assume a two-level signature scheme, which consists of integrated signatures at the higher level and simple signatures at the lower level. Thus, the total number of packets occupied by the signatures is:

$$\text{SIG}_m = \text{SIG}_i + \text{SIG}_s$$

The length of a complete cycle is:

$$\text{CYCLE}_m = \text{SIG}_m + \text{DATA}$$

The average initial probe time is derived based on the probability of the initial probe location and the corresponding probe time:

$$\text{PROBE}_m = \frac{k \cdot n}{k \cdot n + k \cdot r + r} \cdot \frac{n}{2} + \frac{k \cdot r}{k \cdot n + k \cdot r + r} \cdot \left(\frac{r}{2} + n \right) + \frac{r}{k \cdot n + k \cdot r + r} \cdot \frac{r}{2}$$
$$= \frac{k \cdot n^2 + (k+1)r^2 + 2 \cdot k \cdot nr}{2(k \cdot n + (k+1)r)}$$

The access time can be approximated as follows:

$$\text{ACCESS}_m = \text{PROBE}_m + \text{CYCLE}_m$$

The tune-in time in the initial probe period is:

$$
\begin{aligned}
\text{PT}_m &= \frac{k \cdot n}{k \cdot n + k \cdot r + r} \cdot \frac{n}{2} + \frac{k \cdot r}{k \cdot n + k \cdot r + r} \cdot \frac{r}{2} + \frac{r}{k \cdot n + k \cdot r + r} \cdot \frac{r}{2} \\
&= \frac{k \cdot n^2 + (k+1)r^2}{2(k \cdot n + (k+1)r)}
\end{aligned}
$$

To simplify the formula for the estimate of the tune-in time, we assume that the integrated signature for the group of the initial probe is a true match. Therefore, the tune-in time can be approximated as follows:

$$
\begin{aligned}
\text{TUNE}_m = \ &\text{PT}_m + \text{SIG}_i + k \cdot r + k \cdot P_s \cdot n \\
&+ k \cdot P_f^s \cdot n + (I - \lceil P_s \cdot A/l \rceil - 1) \cdot P_f^i \cdot \left(k \cdot r + k \cdot P_f^s \cdot n \right) \\
&+ \lceil P_s \cdot A/l \rceil \left(k \cdot r + l \cdot n + (k-l) \cdot P_f^s \cdot n \right)
\end{aligned}
$$

2.4.4. Comparisons. Using the formulae developed above, we compare the access time and tune-in time of the three schemes. Table 1 lists the parameter values used in the comparisons. In the comparisons, we assume that the selectivity of a query is 1%. For the integrated and multi-level schemes, four information frames are grouped together to generate an integrated signature. The false drop probability for the simple and integrated signatures can be calculated based on m and the number of bit strings superimposed, s_s and s_i. Since the integrated scheme is good for broadcast with similar information frames, we assume that 30% of the superimposed bit strings are overlapped. Therefore, $s_i = 70\% \cdot s_s \cdot 4$. Also, we assume that the locality of frames is three. In other words, for the truly matched integrated signatures, three out of its associated information frames are truly qualified. The same assumption is applied to the multi-level scheme. We vary the signatures length, m, from 1 to 35 packets to observe the changes on access time and tune-in time.

Figure 7 shows that the access times of the three schemes are linearly proportional to the size of the signatures. Since the total size of the information frames is fixed at 10^7 packets, the increase in access time over the signature size represents the overheads of the signature schemes. The choice of the signature size depends on the parameter to be optimized. For instance, document retrieval typically minimizes the number of false drops, meaning that the signature size should be as large as possible—subjected only to the storage overhead affordable—since the false drop probability decreases monotonically with the increase of signature length. On the other hand, the goal of the signature file in information filtering

Table 1. Parameters of the cost models.

$p = 128$	$n = 1000$	$s_s = 100$	$s_i = 280$
$k = 4$	$l = 3$	$A = 10000$	$P_s = 0.01$

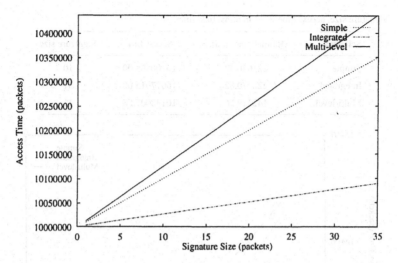

Figure 7.   Access time vs. signature size.

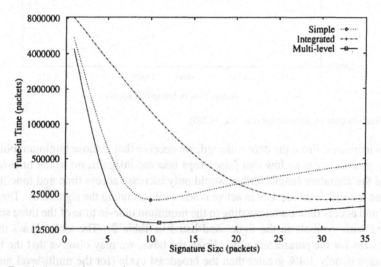

Figure 8.   Tune-in time vs. signature size.

is to minimize the tune-in time. As shown next, there is an optimal signature length which minimizes the tune-in time (from 0.77% of the information frame for the integrated approach to 1.38% of the information frame for the multi-level method).

From figure 7, we also find that the overhead of the multi-level scheme is close to the sum of the overheads for the other two schemes. This is attributed to the fact that the multi-level scheme is a combination of the other two schemes and that the overall size of signatures plays an important role to the increased access time.

Figure 8 shows the tune-in time for the three schemes. From the figure, we may observe that the tune-in time decreases to the minimum and then increases again as the size of the

17

Table 2. Signature size, access time w.r.t. minimal tune time.

Schemes	Minimal tune-in time	Access time	Signature size
Simple	221620.82	10100505.00	10
Integrated	222370.82	10077015.00	31
Multi-level	142319.26	10138007.58	11

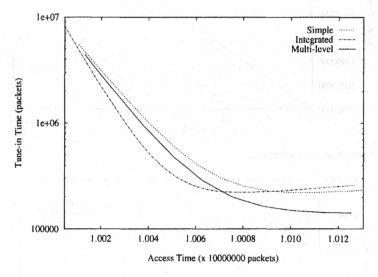

Figure 9. Tune-in time vs. access time ($l = 3$; $s_i = 280$).

signatures increases. From the data collected, we observe that at those minimum points the false drop probability is so low that false drops become insignificant to the tune-in time. Increasing the signature length further would only increase access time and tune-in time, because the mobile client must be in active mode while scanning the signatures. The signature sizes and access time corresponding to the minimum tune-in time of the three schemes are labeled with symbols in the figure and listed in Table 2. The table shows the best signature sizes for the parameters used. From the table, we may observe that the highest access delays is only 1.4% greater than the broadcast cycle (for the multi-level method), while the lowest tune-in time saving is 97.7% (for the integrated method).

Although Table 2 gives us the best choice of the signature sizes for the three schemes, it doesn't give us a fair comparison for the performance among the three schemes. Figure 9 compares the tune-in times in terms of access time. With a given access time, the figure tells the best choice among the three schemes. From the figure, we may come to the conclusion that the integrated scheme and multi-level scheme are better than the simple scheme, while the integrated scheme is the best when access time is small and the multi-level scheme prevails otherwise. However, the performance of the integrated scheme is dependent on the locality in the frame groups and the overlaps among the superimposed bit strings. If the locality is 1 and there is no overlap, the integrated scheme will have a worse tune-in time than the simple scheme due to longer initial probe time and heavy overhead for

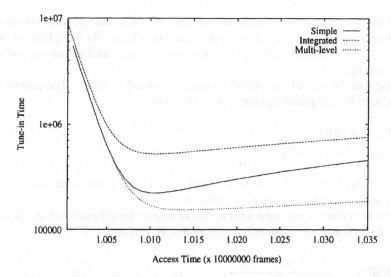

Figure 10.   Tune-in time vs. access time ($l = 1$; $s_i = 400$).

the true match frames (there is no overhead for true matches in simple scheme). In other words, the performance of the integrated scheme is highly dependent on the contents of the information frames and their clustering.

For the multi-level scheme, however, the signatures at the lowest level are indeed simple signatures. We expect the tune-in time of this scheme to be at least as good as the simple scheme with some access time delay for upper level signatures. Therefore, we compare the worst case of the integrated and multi-level schemes (i.e., the locality is 1 and there is no overlap bit strings in a frame group) to the simple scheme. Figure 10 shows that with small access delay (i.e., less than 0.6% of the optimal access time) the tune-in time of the simple scheme and the multi-level scheme is roughly the same. For access delays of more than 0.6% of the optimal access time, the multi-level scheme has a much better tune-in time than the simple scheme.

2.5.   Adaptation of signature sizes

In the previous section, we fixed the size of the signatures used in the multi-level signature scheme. Since the integrated signatures index more information frames than the simple signatures do, the false drop probability of the integrated signatures is higher than that of the simple signatures. On one hand, since the integrated signatures are more frequently used in filtering than the simple signatures, it is desirable to lower their false drop probability by increasing the signature length in order to reduce further matching of the associated simple signatures. On the other hand, lengthening the integrated signatures will increase the tune-in time and also the access time.

In this section, we fix the total overhead of the signatures and adjust the ratio of the storage occupied by the simple and integrated signatures in order to observe the minimal

19

tune-in time for the multi-level signature scheme. To be consistent with our discussion in previous session, we assume a two-level signature scheme. In the following, we use subscripts i and s to distinguish the symbols used for integrated signatures and simple signatures, respectively.

Assume that the size of the overall signature overhead is SIG_m. The portion of the overhead used for integrated signatures is q. Therefore,

$$\mathrm{SIG}_i = q \cdot \mathrm{SIG}_m$$
$$\mathrm{SIG}_s = (1 - q) \cdot \mathrm{SIG}_m$$

As a result, the numbers of packets allocated for each integrated signature and simple signature are: $r_i = \lfloor \mathrm{SIG}_i / I \rfloor$ and $r_s = \lfloor \mathrm{SIG}_s / A \rfloor$.

The cost formulae for the multi-level signature scheme are reformulated as follows. We only list the formulae which are different from that in Section 2.4.3.

$$\mathrm{PROBE}_m = \frac{k \cdot (n + r_s)^2 + r_i^2}{2(k \cdot n + k \cdot r_s + r_i)}$$

The tune-in time in the initial probe period is:

$$\mathrm{PT}_m = \frac{k \cdot n^2 + k \cdot r_s^2 + r_i^2}{2(k \cdot n + k \cdot r_s + r_i)}$$

The tune-in time is as follows.

$$\begin{aligned}
\mathrm{TUNE}_m = {} & \mathrm{PT}_m + \mathrm{SIG}_i + k \cdot r_s + k \cdot P_s \cdot n + k \cdot P_f^s \cdot n \\
& + (I - \lceil P_s \cdot A / l \rceil - 1) \cdot P_f^i \cdot (k \cdot r_s + k \cdot P_f^s \cdot n) \\
& + \lceil P_s \cdot A / l \rceil (k \cdot r_s + l \cdot n + (k - l) \cdot P_f^s \cdot n)
\end{aligned}$$

2.5.1. Comparison.

Based on the cost models we developed above, we like to see the change in tune-in time based on different ratios between the integrated and simple signatures. Figure 11 shows the tune-in time with respect to the share of the total signature overhead that the integrated signatures occupy, q, given that the total signature overhead is 100,000 packets. We increase q from 0 to 1 by 1% each time. From the figure, the minimal tune-in time is at $q = 0.3$. In other words, when 30% of the total signature overhead are used for the integrated signatures, the tune-in time is the lowest. In this case, the sizes of the integrated and simple signatures are 12 and 7 packets per signature, respectively. However, the minimal point may change when a different total signature overhead is used. Since packets have fixed size, the allocated signature space must be truncated to fit into an integral number of packets. This situation can also be observed from the zig-zag behavior in figure 11.

Figure 12 compares, based on the same access time, the tune-in time of the "optimized" multi-level signature scheme and the original multi-level signature scheme (which has the same signature length for the integrated and simple signatures). In this experiment, we set

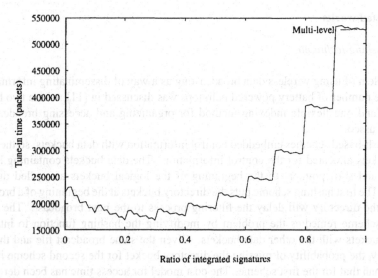

Figure 11. Tune-in time vs. integrated signature share.

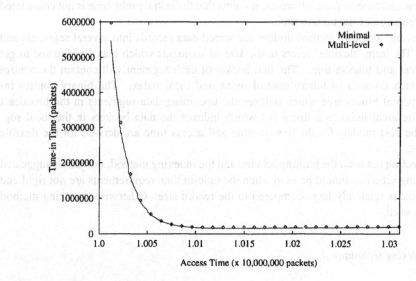

Figure 12. Minimal tune-in time vs. access time.

the size of frame group to 15. Other experiments with different frame group sizes have similar results. We observe that although the performance of the original configuration is not as good as the optimized one, the gap is quite insignificant. Therefore, one may choose to adopt the original configuration for the simplicity of signature generation and comparison.

3. Related works

3.1. Hashing technique

The problem of using wireless data broadcasting as a way of disseminating information to a massive number of battery powered palmtops was discussed in [11], where two hashing schemes and one flexible indexing method for organizing and accessing broadcast data were discussed.

The hash-based schemes embedded control information with data buckets, so there is no extra buckets allocated for the control information. The data buckets containing hashing function and shift pointers to the beginning of the logical buckets are called directory buckets. The first hashing scheme puts the directory buckets at the beginning of a broadcast. Missing the directory will delay the filtering process to the next broadcast. The second hashing scheme remedies the problem by modifying the hashing function to interleave control buckets with the other data buckets. Given the same broadcast file and the same search key, the probability of missing the directory bucket for the second scheme is much smaller than that for the first scheme. The cost model for access time has been derived for the hashing schemes. However, the tune-in time is not analysed. There is a table of data for access time and tune-in time. However, it seems that the initial probe time is not considered in the calculation of the tune-in time.

The flexible indexing method divides the sorted data records into several segments and indexes. The term 'flexible' refers to the size of segments which may be adjusted to get good access and tune-in time. The first bucket of each segment will contain the control index, which consists of binary control index and local index. The binary control index is a partial binary tree which indexes the upcoming data segments in the broadcast cycle. The local index is a linear list which indexes the data buckets in the local segment. The cost models for the tune-in time and access time are derived for the flexible index.

On selecting between the hashing scheme and the indexing method, the author suggested that hashing schemes should be used when the tune-in time requirements are not rigid and the key size is relatively large compared to the record size. Otherwise, indexing method should be used.

3.2. Indexing technique

Two methods, $(1, m)$ indexing and distributed indexing, for organizing and accessing broadcast data were described in [12]. The paper assumes that the queries are based on the primary key. The data frames are sorted by the primary key. Also, the paper assumes that the size of the data is small enough to fit into a frame.

In the $(1, m)$ indexing method, a tree-structured index, e.g., B^+-Tree, is created for the data frames in the broadcast cycle. The data frames are divided into m segments. A replication of the index, called the index segment, is created for each data segment. After accessing the index, the mobile client may enter doze mode and wake up when the data frame arrives.

The distributed indexing is based on the observation that there is no need to replicate the entire index between successive data segments. For each data segment, there is an index segment which consists of two parts: the replicated part indexes different data segments and the non-replicated part indexes the data buckets in a data segment.

The cost models for the tune-in time and the access time are derived for both $(1, m)$ indexing and distributed indexing method.

3.3. Broadcast disks

Acharya et al. [1] proposed *broadcast disks* for mobile clients. The broadcast disk super-imposes multiple information streams into a super-stream for broadcasting on one single channel. The idea is to interleave the information frames of different streams at some spec-ified frequencies. The information frames from the more important streams are broadcast more often than those from less important streams. Thus, the frequencies of various streams may be adjusted to reflect the user demands.

In addition to showing how to superimpose information streams into a broadcast channel, the paper discussed caching techniques for broadcast disks. Due to the serial and shared nature of information broadcasting, two new caching policies, PIX and LIX , are proposed. Instead of caching the hottest pages, the policies are based on the ratio of local access probability to broadcast frequency. In other words, if the hottest frames may easily be obtained on the air, they need not be cached. The best candidates for caching are those accessed frequently but difficult to obtain. PIX is not an implementable policy, because it's based on the access probabilities of frames in a mobile client. Thus, LIX is modified from LRU by taking into account of the broadcast frequencies to approximate PIX. In [21], the same authors also discussed the prefetch strategies of caching for broadcast disks. However, the results are not conclusive.

4. Conclusion

Since most queries on broadcast information select only a small number of information frames, indexing is very effective in reducing the tune-in time. With a reasonable false drop probability and small signature overhead, the signature schemes is excellent for information filtering in information broadcast services. Compared to traditional indexing, the signature method is particularly suitable for mobile clients because it can perform realtime filtering with little processing and memory requirement.

This paper discusses the application of signature techniques to information filtering. We propose three signature schemes, namely simple signature, integrated signature and multi-level signature schemes. We also analyse the impact of the ratio between integrated signa-tures and simple signatures on optimizing tune-in time for the multi-level signature scheme.

Unlike the performance consideration of traditional disk accesses, tune-in time, corre-sponding to battery consumption in the operation, and access time are used as performance criteria in evaluating our signature designs. The cost models for the tune-in time and access time of each of the signature schemes have been developed and compared based on various factors.

The result shows that, with fixed signature size, the multi-level scheme has the best tune-in time performance but has the longest access time; the integrated scheme has the best average access time, but its tune-in time depends on the similarity among the information frames; the simple scheme has a fair access time and tune-in time. Compared to a broadcast channel without any indexing, all of the three schemes improve tune-in time performance dramatically with a reasonable access time overhead.

For future research, we will investigate caching policies for caches of fixed size and optimization issues involved with data and channel allocation when mobile clients are capable of transmitting queries to the central server.

References

1. S. Acharya, R. Alonso, M. Franklin, and S. Zdonik, "Broadcast disks: Data management for asymmetric communication environments," Department of Computer Science, Brown University, Technical Report No. CS-94-43, December 1994.
2. R. Alonso and S. Ganguly, "Energy efficient query optimization," Matsushita Information Technology Laboratory, MITL-TR-33-92, November 1992.
3. A. Asthana, M. Cravatts, and P. Krzyzanowski, "An indoor wireless system for personalized shopping assistance," MOBIDATA: An Interactive Journal of Mobile Computing, vol. 1, no. 1, 1994.
4. N. Ballard, "Nigel Ballard's MINI PDA comparison chart #47," Nigel Ballard Bournemouth, U.K., http://www.eit.com/mailinglists/zoomer/documents/pda.html, February 1994.
5. B. Barriginer, T. Burd, F. Burghardt, A. Burstein, A. Chandrakasan, R. Doering, S. Narayanaswamy, T. Pering, B. Richards, T. Truman, J. Rabaey, and R. Brodersen, "Infopad: A system design for wireless multimedia access," Wireless94, Calgary, July 1994.
6. T.D. Burd and R.W. Brodersen, "Energy efficient CMOS microprocessor design," Proceedings of the Twenty-Eighth Hawaii International Conference on System Sciences, 1995, pp. 288–297.
7. W.W. Chang and H.J. Schek, "A signature access method for the starburst database system," Proceedings of the Fifteenth International Conference on Very Large Data Bases, Amsterdam, The Netherlands, August 1989, pp. 145–153.
8. C. Faloutsos and S. Christodoulakis, "Signature files: An access method for documents and its analytical performance evaluation," ACM Transactions on Office Information Systems, vol. 2, no. 4, pp. 267–288, 1984.
9. S. Ganguly and R. Alonso, "Query optimization in mobile environments," Department of Computer Science, Rutgers University, LCSR-TR-219, 1993.
10. T. Imielinski and B.R. Badrinath, "Mobile wireless computing: Solutions and challenges in data management," Department of Computer Science, Rutgers University, DCS-TR-296, 1993.
11. T. Imielinski, S. Viswanathan, and B.R. Badrinath, "Power efficiency filtering of data on air," Proceedings of the International Conference on Extending Database Technology, 1994, pp. 245–258.
12. T. Imielinski, S. Viswanathan, and B.R. Badrinath, "Energy efficiency indexing on air," Proceedings of the International Conference on SIGMOD, May 1994, pp. 25–36.
13. D.L. Lee, Y.M. Kim, and G. Patel, "Efficient signature file methods for text retrieval," IEEE Transactions on Data and Knowledge Engineering, vol. 7, no. 3, pp. 423–435, 1995.
14. S.-Y. Lee, M.-C. Yang, and J.-W. Chen, "Signature file as a spatial filter for iconic image database," Journal of Visual Languages and Computing, vol. 3, no. 4, pp. 373–397, 1992.
15. W.-C. Lee and D.L. Lee, "Using signature and caching techniques for information filtering in wireless and mobile environments," Department of Computer Science, University of Science and Technology, Technical Report HKUST-CS96-2, Hong Kong, January 1996.
16. F. Rabitti and P. Zezula, "A dynamic signature technique for multimedia databases," Proceedings of the 13th International Conference on Research and Development in Information Retrieval, September 1990, pp. 193–210.

17. S. Shekhar and D.-R. Liu, "Genesis and advanced traveler information systems (ATIS): Killer applications for mobile computing?," MOBIDATA: An Interactive Journal of Mobile Computing, vol. 1, no. 1, 1994.
18. S. Stiassny, "Mathematical analysis of various superimposed coding methods," American Documentation, vol. 11, no. 2, pp. 155–169, 1960.
19. P. Tiberio and P. Zezula, "Selecting signature files for specific applications," Information Processing and Management, vol. 29, no. 4, pp. 487–498, 1993.
20. Wireless Data Group, "Envoy: personal wireless communicator," Motorola Inc., Brochure, July 1994.
21. S. Zdonik, M. Franklin, R. Alonso, and S. Acharya, "Are 'Disk in the Air' Just Pie in the Sky?," Proceedings of IEEE Workshop on Mobile Computing Systmes and Applications, Santa Cruz, December 1994, pp. 12–19.

Distributed and Parallel Databases, 4, 229–247 (1996)

Exotica/FMDC: A Workflow Management System for Mobile and Disconnected Clients

G. ALONSO   alonso@inf.ethz.ch
Department of Computer Science, ETH-Zürich, ETH-Zentrum, CH-8092 Zürich, Switzerland

R. GÜNTHÖR   rgunthor@heidelbg.ibm.com
IBM European Networking Center, Postfach 10 30 68, 69020 Heidelberg, Germany

M. KAMATH   kamath@cs.umass.edu
Department of Computer Science, University of Massachusetts, Amherst, MA 01003, USA

D. AGRAWAL, A. EL ABBADI   {agrawal,amr}@cs.ucsb.edu
Department of Computer Science, University of California, Santa Barbara, CA 93106, USA

C. MOHAN   mohan@almaden.ibm.com
IBM Almaden Research Center, 650 Harry Road, San Jose, CA 95120, USA

Received May 1, 1995; Accepted February 12, 1996

Recommended by: Daniel Barbara, Ravi Jain, Narayanan Krishnakumar

Abstract. Workflow Management Systems (WFMSs) automate the execution of business processes in environments encompassing large numbers of users distributed over a wide geographic area and using heterogeneous resources. Current implementations allow the definition and controlled execution of complex and long lived business processes as the basis for an enterprise-wide collaborative system but, in most cases, the autonomy of the users is greatly restricted due to architectural and design considerations. In particular, existing systems are built around a centralized server. As a result, users need to maintain an uninterrupted connection with the server to perform the different tasks assigned to them. This is a severe restriction, especially when considering the emergence of mobile computing, and the increase in use of laptops and small computers which are connected to the network only occasionally and which will, undoubtedly, be the tool of choice for many users. This paper addresses the problem of supporting disconnected workflow clients in large workflow management systems while still preserving the correctness of the overall execution and allowing coordinated interactions between the different users regardless of their location.

Keywords: Workflow, Disconnected Operation, Mobile Computing

1. Introduction

Workflow Management Systems, WFMSs, are seen as a key tool to improve the efficiency of an organization by automating the execution of its business processes. A WFMS supports the modeling, coordinated execution and monitoring of the activities that take place within an organization. It is up to the user to define such activities and organize them in the most efficient way using the tools provided by business process re-engineering [13], but once the activities and processes of interest have been defined, the workflow management system is used to represent the business processes and to assign the staff and role hierarchies in the organization within which those business processes will be executed. During the execution of the business process, the workflow management system acts as a coordinator: the WFMS delivers the various tasks to each user, collects results, determines the next steps, controls the activities of each user, and detects when the process has successfully terminated. The patterns of collaboration among the users are predefined as dependencies between individual steps within a business process, with each step being assigned to potentially different users. Thus, the synergy between all the steps is provided by the designer of the business process. Note that full automation is not possible, since human intervention is necessary to solve many crucial steps and to determine what to do in case of errors and unpredictable events. However, the use of a workflow management system simplifies to a great extent the task of coordinating large numbers of users working in heterogeneous and distributed environments.

Many existing WFMSs are built based on a client-server architecture due to the simplicity of the design and the synchronization problems posed by other architectures [4, 3]. Such an approach has many advantages and it is useful in many organizations where the server is installed in some central computer and users access the system through terminals, PCs or workstations, installed in their offices. Most clerical work, form processing, accounting activities, and stock management, to name a few applications, is done this way. However, there are many other applications where this may not be the best approach.

Recently, *disconnected operation* has been identified as one of the main ways in which computers will be used in the future [17]. Taking advantage of the arrival of more reliable and powerful portable and home desktop computers, users within an organization can work independently of the main computer facilities: applications and data are loaded in the laptops or desktops by briefly connecting with a server, the connection is broken, and users work locally on those applications and data. After the work has been completed, which may be in a few hours or few days, users reconnect with the server and transfer the results of their work. Disconnected operation offers many obvious advantages but, in many ways, disconnected computing and workflow management systems have contradictory goals. A workflow management system is a tool for cooperation and collaborative work in which users work within a preestablished framework that guarantees progress towards a certain goal, the business process, of which the users may not be aware. This requires constant monitoring and checking of the users' activities. On the other hand, disconnected computing is geared towards supporting users who work in isolation from other users. There is not much room for collaboration in disconnected mode.

This paper addresses the problem of supporting disconnected clients in a large workflow management system. The goal is to give enough autonomy to the clients to allow them to perform work without having to be connected to the rest of the system and still maintain the overall correctness and consistency of the processes being executed. To bridge the gap between disconnection and coordination, we propose a compromise between both worlds. Users must "commit" themselves to perform certain tasks before disconnecting from the system. The workflow management system takes advantage of such commitment to assign tasks to users, allowing them to work on their own while ensuring overall correctness and constant progress towards the goal of the business process. The ideas described in this paper is one of the first studies on the impact of portable computers on collaborative workflow

BIOLOGICALLY-INSPIRED COLLABORATIVE COMPUTING

IFIP – The International Federation for Information Processing

IFIP was founded in 1960 under the auspices of UNESCO, following the First World Computer Congress held in Paris the previous year. An umbrella organization for societies working in information processing, IFIP's aim is two-fold: to support information processing within its member countries and to encourage technology transfer to developing nations. As its mission statement clearly states,

> IFIP's mission is to be the leading, truly international, apolitical organization which encourages and assists in the development, exploitation and application of information technology for the benefit of all people.

IFIP is a non-profitmaking organization, run almost solely by 2500 volunteers. It operates through a number of technical committees, which organize events and publications. IFIP's events range from an international congress to local seminars, but the most important are:

• The IFIP World Computer Congress, held every second year;
• Open conferences;
• Working conferences.

The flagship event is the IFIP World Computer Congress, at which both invited and contributed papers are presented. Contributed papers are rigorously refereed and the rejection rate is high.

As with the Congress, participation in the open conferences is open to all and papers may be invited or submitted. Again, submitted papers are stringently refereed.

The working conferences are structured differently. They are usually run by a working group and attendance is small and by invitation only. Their purpose is to create an atmosphere conducive to innovation and development. Refereeing is less rigorous and papers are subjected to extensive group discussion.

Publications arising from IFIP events vary. The papers presented at the IFIP World Computer Congress and at open conferences are published as conference proceedings, while the results of the working conferences are often published as collections of selected and edited papers.

Any national society whose primary activity is in information may apply to become a full member of IFIP, although full membership is restricted to one society per country. Full members are entitled to vote at the annual General Assembly, National societies preferring a less committed involvement may apply for associate or corresponding membership. Associate members enjoy the same benefits as full members, but without voting rights. Corresponding members are not represented in IFIP bodies. Affiliated membership is open to non-national societies, and individual and honorary membership schemes are also offered.

systems [2, 5], and the first to provide a feasible solution where the implementation aspects are discussed within the constraints of a real system. For this purpose, we use FlowMark [18, 19], a workflow product from IBM that uses a client-server architecture, where the ideas described here have been implemented.

The rest of the paper is organized as follows. Section 2 presents the basic ideas behind workflow systems pointing out the architectural and conceptual problems to support disconnected operation. Section 3 describes the functioning of the system when clients are connected to the system at all times. Section 4 discusses possible solutions for supporting disconnected clients in terms of three different phases. Section 5 addresses the problem of locating clients in the system when they are mobile and can connect to different servers. Section 6 discusses some of the issues raised in previous sections and the implemented prototype. Section 7 summarizes related work and Section 8 concludes the paper.

2. Workflow Systems

This section introduces the basic concepts of workflow management according to the definitions provided by the *Workflow Management Coalition*, *WfMC*, in its *Reference Model* [14, 22]. The WfMC is an international organization leading the efforts to standardize workflow management products. Implementation details are discussed based on FlowMark [18, 19], IBM's workflow product.

2.1. Business Processes and Workflow Management Systems

The reference model defines a *business process* as "a procedure where documents, information or tasks are passed between participants according to defined sets of rules to achieve, or contribute to, an overall business goal" [14]. An example of a business process is shown in Figure 1. Some of the steps within a process may also be complex processes themselves. For instance, in Figure 1, *Case study* and *Finalize credit* are shown as nested processes. From this definition, it is easy to see the contradictory goals of automating the execution of business processes and providing support for disconnected operation. The key idea in any workflow system is to pass "documents, information or tasks" around the participants (as *forms* [29], *electronic mail* [12, 23], or transactional activities [11, 27, 30], for instance), while disconnected operation is geared towards user's autonomy.

A business process can be expressed as a schematic representation of the procedural knowledge related to certain activities. This is generally called a *workflow*. Hence, a *workflow management system*, WFMS, is "a system that completely defines, manages and executes workflows through the execution of software whose order of execution is driven by a computer representation of the workflow logic" [14]. Once again, note that a WFMS automates the execution of workflows, which are representations of business processes and, hence, "automation" acquires different meanings depending on the type of processes. For business processes in general, this automation involves performing several tasks: scheduling activities, mapping activities to users currently in the system, tracking the progress of activities, assigning resources to activities, and so forth. In existing systems these tasks are

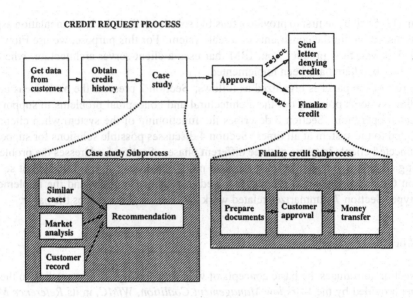

Figure 1. A Loan Request as an Example of a Business Process

all performed by the server, hence, to accommodate disconnected clients, some modifications to the overall system design will be necessary to guarantee progress without clients having to access the server at each step.

2.2. *Workflow Model*

The Workflow Management Coalition defines a *process* as a coordinated set of activities connected in order to achieve a common goal [22]. The automated components of such a process forms a *workflow process*. For simplicity, in what follows we will use the term process to refer to a workflow process, i.e., we will assume a process can be automated in its entirety. A *process* consists of *activities* and *relevant data*. Activities are the different steps of the process and associated with each of them is an *invoked application*, the application to execute, and a *role*, the set of users responsible for the execution of the activity. The *invoked application* can be a computer program or a human activity. The *relevant data* is defined as the data being transferred among activities. The flow of control within a process, i.e., what to execute next, is determined by *transition conditions*, usually boolean expressions based on relevant data. Users are represented in terms of *roles*, and activities are generally associated to roles instead of individual users. This allows the system to determine who is currently available and assign the activity to that user instead of having to wait until an individual user logs on. The invoked applications can be almost anything as long as there is a way to communicate their result to the WFMS. In the case of applications being programs, *Application Program Interface*, API, calls are used to access and return data.

One of the most relevant aspects of a WFMS is the use of *worklists*. Worklists can be seen as the interface of the WFMS to the end user. A worklist is a list of workitems associated with a particular user, and each user has one. Each workitem is an activity that belongs to a process being executed and that has been assigned to this user, and possibly also to others with the same role, for its completion. Hence, the same activity may appear in several worklists at the same time. In this case, when an activity is selected in one worklist, it will be deleted from all other worklists. The mapping between roles, users, activities and worklists is automatically performed by the system. All this functionality must be maintained during disconnected operation.

2.3. Workflow System Architectures

WFMSs have various possible architectures [3], but for the purposes of this paper they all have similar characteristics. In general, the functionality of a workflow system is distributed among three different components: *runtime control, runtime interactions* and *buildtime* [14]. Runtime control has two aspects to it: *persistent storage* and *process navigation*. Persistent storage allows the system to recover from failures without losing data and also provides the means to maintain an audit trail of the execution of processes. The navigational logic controls the execution of processes. Thus, we consider two components within runtime control, the *storage server* and the *navigation server*. These are referred to as the Workflow control data and the Workflow Engine in the reference model. Similarly, runtime interactions are of two types, with the users and with invoked applications. The former is the interface with the end users and consist mainly of the worklist assigned to a given user. The latter is the interface to the applications being executed as part of a workflow. We consider them as separate components, the *User Interface* and the *Application Interface*. These appear in the reference model as *Worklist* and *Invoked Applications*. We will not discuss the details of buildtime operations since they are somewhat orthogonal to the actual execution of processes.

2.4. FlowMark's Model and Architecture

The reference model does not provide any guidance in terms of implementation and lacks a detailed description of the interactions between the different components. For this purpose we use FlowMark, an IBM product which closely follows the reference model. Except for some minor implementation differences, the ideas described in the rest of the paper should apply to any WFMS that follows the functional specifications of the Workflow Coalition reference model.

Business processes are modeled in FlowMark as acyclic directed graphs in which nodes represent steps of execution and edges represent the flow of control and data [18, 19]. The main components of FlowMark's *workflow model* are: *processes, activities, control connectors, data connectors,* and *conditions*. A process is a description of the sequence of steps involved in accomplishing a given goal and it is represented as a graph. Activities are the nodes in the process graph and represent the steps to be completed. Control connectors

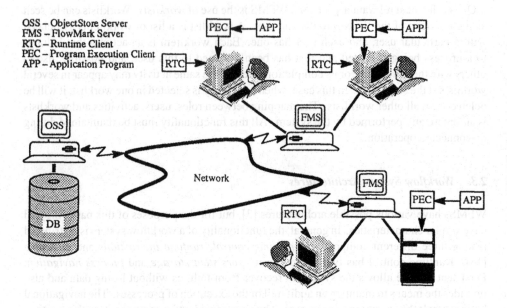

OSS – ObjectStore Server
FMS – FlowMark Server
RTC – Runtime Client
PEC – Program Execution Client
APP – Application Program

Figure 2. Runtime Components of FlowMark

are used to specify the order of execution between activities and are represented as directed edges in the process graph. Data connectors specify the flow of information from one activity to another in the form of mappings between the data containers of the activities and are also expressed as directed edges in the process graph. Each activity has one *input data container* and one *output data container*. Finally, conditions specify when certain events will happen. There are three types of conditions: *transition conditions* associated with control connectors determine whether the connector evaluates to true or false; *start conditions*, which specify when an activity will be started; and *exit conditions*, used to specify when an activity is considered to have terminated.

In terms of its architecture, FlowMark runs across different platforms (AIX, OS/2, Windows) and supports distribution of most of its components. However, in its current version, persistent data resides in a single database server, ObjectStore. This has facilitated the design of the overall system, but introduces a single point of failure in the architecture [1]. As far as we know, existing systems such as Wang's *OPEN/Workflow*, AT&T's *ProcessIT*, Fujitsu's *Regatta*, XSoft's *InConcert*, or Action Technologies' *Action Workflow* are also based on a centralized repository and, hence, suffer from the same problem. Besides the database server, FlowMark is organized into three other components: *FlowMark Server*, *Runtime Client* and *Buildtime Client* as shown in Figure 2. These correspond to the three functionalities mentioned in the reference model: Buildtime Client for buildtime functions, Runtime Client for runtime interactions, and FlowMark Server for runtime control.

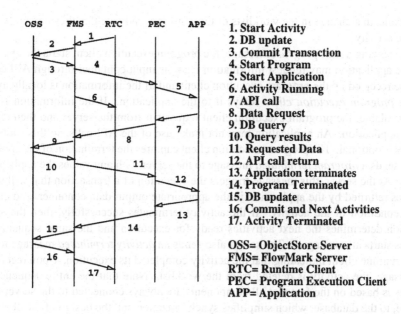

OSS	FMS	RTC	PEC	APP

1. Start Activity
2. DB update
3. Commit Transaction
4. Start Program
5. Start Application
6. Activity Running
7. API call
8. Data Request
9. DB query
10. Query results
11. Requested Data
12. API call return
13. Application terminates
14. Program Terminated
15. DB update
16. Commit and Next Activities
17. Activity Terminated

OSS= ObjectStore Server
FMS= FlowMark Server
RTC= Runtime Client
PEC= Program Execution Client
APP= Application

Figure 3. Message Exchange Between FlowMark Components During the Execution of an Activity

3. Normal Operation with Continuous Connection to the Server

In FlowMark, a running process is called a *process instance*, and there can be many instances of the same process running concurrently. An activity can be executed automatically (programs) or manually by a human role. We focus only on manual activities since only they are interesting in the disconnected context. When an activity of a process instance becomes ready for execution, FlowMark first performs role and staff resolution to determine all the users who are eligible to execute the activity. It then updates the worklists of all these users by including the activity as a new workitem. For all of those users who are logged onto FlowMark, an *activity ready* message is sent to their corresponding runtime clients.

The complete exchange of messages that occurs among the different components when an activity is executed, shown in Figure 3, is as follows: once the *activity ready* message arrives at a runtime client, the activity is displayed in the user's worklist. When the user selects the activity from the worklist, the runtime client sends a *start activity* message to the server. Upon receiving such a message, the workflow server initiates a transaction on the database to retrieve the necessary information to execute the application that corresponds to the activity. This includes the node where it has to be executed, the access path, permissions required, user-id, program name, and so forth. With this information, the server determines the program execution client that will execute the application and sends to it a *start program* message. The server also sends an *activity running* message to the runtime client that will result in the status of the activity being changed in the worklist. Finally, the server notifies all other users who were eligible to execute the activity that the activity is already executing, which results in a change in the worklists of these users to indicate that they can no longer select the activity.

Upon receiving a *start program* message, the program execution client starts the application. The application may request information from its input container through API calls. These are received by the program execution client and, if the information is locally available, the *program execution client* relays it to the application. If the information is not locally available, the program execution client requests it from the server and then relays it to the application. An application may not make use of the API calls, so this round of messages is optional. The program execution client captures the termination of the application and sends a *program terminated* message to the server with any values the application returned. At the server, this message triggers the execution of a transaction that will store the values returned by the application in the appropriate output data container, and check the exit condition of the activity. If the activity terminates successfully, then the same transaction determines the next activities ready for execution and the same sequence of messages starts all over again. The server also sends an *activity terminated* message to the original runtime client indicating that the activity completed its execution. Upon receiving this message, the activity is deleted from the worklist. Note that the entire sequence of messages is based on the fact that all components are always connected to the server and, therefore, to the database, which simplifies synchronization and the design of the clients.

4. Supporting Disconnected Clients

Support for disconnected operation can be provided in two ways, one is to have the clients working in a "batch" mode, where a set of activities is assigned to them and all the relevant information is downloaded to the clients prior to their disconnection. The other is to allow the clients to perform navigation themselves by transferring entire parts of a process to the clients. It turns out that the latter option adds significant overhead to the design since it requires to duplicate at the clients much of the functionality of the server. Thus, we have chosen the "batch" mode as the most viable option.

4.1. Process Execution During Disconnection

For simplicity, we rule out from our model disconnections due to failures. In what follows, we will assume that disconnection is a voluntary step taken by the user and that this is declared to the system beforehand. This is not a very restrictive assumption since such an intention can be easily triggered by the user when declaring that some work is to be loaded in the client, a common procedure with portable computers. Such a procedure is known as a *planned* disconnection in the mobile computing literature.

During disconnected operation we will assume that both the runtime client and the program execution client are local, while other components are remote. Runtime clients in FlowMark play a passive role. They are mere interfaces for the user to specify actions such as *start activity*. As such, the role of a runtime client does not change in disconnected mode except for the fact that instead of sending the commands to the centralized database, in disconnected

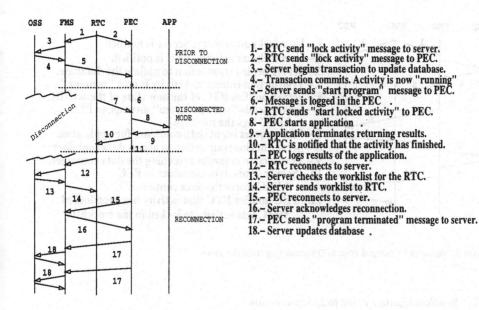

OSS   FMS   RTC   PEC   APP

PRIOR TO
DISCONNECTION

DISCONNECTED
MODE

RECONNECTION

1.– RTC send "lock activity" message to server.
2.– RTC sends "lock activity" message to PEC.
3.– Server begins transaction to update database.
4.– Transaction commits. Activity is now "running"
5.– Server sends "start program" message to PEC.
6.– Message is logged in the PEC .
7.– RTC sends "start locked activity" to PEC.
8.– PEC starts application .
9.– Application terminates returning results.
10.– RTC is notified that the activity has finished.
11.– PEC logs results of the application.
12.– RTC reconnects to server.
13.– Server checks the worklist for the RTC.
14.– Server sends worklist to RTC.
15.– PEC reconnects to server.
16.– Server acknowledges reconnection.
17.– PEC sends "program terminated" message to server.
18.– Server updates database .

Figure 4. Message Exchange Between the Different FlowMark Components During Disconnected Operation

mode it will send them to the program execution client. Similarly, the termination of an activity will not be reported by the database but by the program execution client. Thus, for all practical purposes, the runtime client does not change, except for some added functionality that will be discussed later. The program execution client, during disconnected operation, will act according to the messages received from the runtime client as opposed to reacting to the messages sent from the server. Since it cannot connect to the database to provide additional information requested by the application through API calls, it must also provide its own persistent storage for the information that may be requested by the application. Similarly, it must also persistently store the results of the application's execution until they can be sent to the server.

To accomplish all these changes, we distinguish three phases in the disconnected operation process. The first is a *synchronization* phase in which, prior to disconnection, a user declares the intention to reserve an activity. If it is an activity that can be executed by several users, then the other users are notified that they are no longer eligible to execute the activity. This phase also involves transferring all the information pertaining to the activity from the server to the program execution client. The second phase is the disconnected operation *per se*, in which the user works on the reserved activities without any control from the server. The third phase is the *reconnection* to the server, in which the worklist of the user is updated, and the results of the executions of the activities are reported back to the server for storage in the database. The actual sequence of messages exchanged during these three phases is summarized in Figure 4.

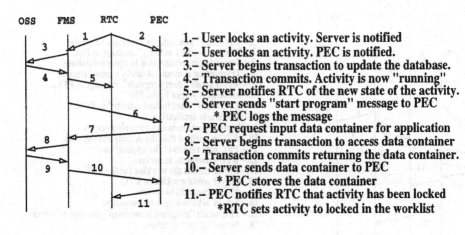

Figure 5. Messages Exchanged Prior to Disconnecting from the Server

4.2. Synchronization Prior to Disconnection

The main purpose of the synchronization phase is to get all participants to "agree" with the disconnection of a given user. During this phase there are two important steps: *locking* and *preloading* the activities that will be available at the client while being disconnected. Locking is necessary due to the fact that the same activities may appear in several worklists simultaneously. Under normal circumstances, the centralized database serializes all changes to an activity and, hence, even if two users attempt to start the same activity concurrently, only one of them will be able to register in the database as the user to which the activity has been assigned. To prevent other users from working concurrently on the same activity, before a user can disconnect from the server, all activities they intend to work on must be *locked* by the user. When a user locks an activity, this implies an explicit commitment to work on that activity, regardless of whether the user works on the activities while connected to the server or disconnected from it. A locked activity is permanently assigned to a user until the user completes it or unlocks it. During disconnected operation only locked activities will appear in the worklist of the user. An activity in the worklist can enter the locked state only from the ready state: activities already running cannot be locked. The server only allows the locking and downloading of activities that can completely run on the mobile client, i.e., not those which need to access a program or database located on a remote machine.

Locking only requires changes to the runtime and program execution clients. Upon receiving a request to lock an activity, the server treats the request as if it were a *start activity* message and behaves accordingly. At the program execution client, however, a *locked activity* is not to be executed immediately. Instead, all the information is stored persistently for later retrieval. At the runtime client, the worklist will change the status of the activity to reflect the fact that it has been locked.

To facilitate the identification of locked activities and minimize the changes at the server, when a user locks an activity, the runtime client sends a *lock activity* message to both the server and the program execution client. To avoid race conditions, the runtime client will have to send the message first to the program execution client, and once it receives an acknowledgement, send the same message to the server. In this way, the server sends the information in exactly the same way as if it were an activity to be executed under normal circumstances and yet the program execution client is able to differentiate between a locked activity and other types of activities.

The program execution client keeps a list of locked activities. When a *start program* message arrives, it is matched against all entries in the worklist. If the application to be executed corresponds to a locked activity, instead of starting the application, the message is stored for later use. Note that this first message contains only the information necessary to start the execution of the program. If the program uses API calls to request information during disconnected operation, more information needs to be retrieved from the database. For this reason, the program execution client also requests from the server the input data container of the locked activity, to be stored with the information of the first message. Once all this is done, the program execution client notifies the runtime client, which then considers the activity to be successfully locked. The exchange of messages is shown in Figure 5.

4.3. *Disconnected Operation*

One of the goals of our design is to maintain the "look and feel" of the interface. From the user's point of view there should not be any difference between normal and disconnected operation, beyond the limitation that during disconnected operation the worklist contains only locked activities. Locked activities behave the same way as standard activities: the user can start the execution of a locked activity, or force its termination. However, this will result in a series of messages exchanged between the runtime client and the program execution client, instead of using the server as an intermediate step.

When the user starts a locked activity, the runtime client sends a *start locked activity* message to the program execution client. Upon receiving this message, the program execution client retrieves the data from its own repository and proceeds as usual when executing an application. Since the input data container of the activity is available at the program execution client when the execution starts, API calls to request data from the container can be satisfied from the program execution client itself.

When the execution of an application terminates, the values it returns are captured by the program execution client. Under normal circumstances, the program execution client would send this data to the server immediately. During disconnected operation, however, this is not possible and, hence, it must store the results until it is reconnected to the server. The termination of the application is also notified to the runtime client which will remove the locked activity from the worklist. However, the runtime client still keeps the name of the activity in a list of locked activities that have been completed. The reason for this will become clear when discussing the reconnection phase. The program execution client can store the messages that will be sent to the server in a sequential manner. No index is necessary since this information will only be accessed once, and the message order is irrelevant.

In FlowMark, the *exit condition* of an activity is used to determine whether the activity has been successfully completed. This exit condition needs to be transferred to the program execution client, along with all the other information related to the activity. The program execution client can then check the condition and determine if the activity has been completed or it needs to be rescheduled again. In the former case it behaves as explained above. In the latter case, the runtime client is notified and the activity will reappear in the worklist as being ready for execution.

4.4. Reconnecting to the Server

When reconnecting to the server, both the runtime client and the program execution client log onto the server as they do in the current version of FlowMark. The registration procedure allows the server to keep track of which clients are available, i.e., who are the users in the system and what program execution clients are available. During normal operation, when the runtime client logs onto the server, the server sends the worklist corresponding to the user of that runtime client. The new worklist contains all activities locked previous to disconnection, all activities that were already there but were not locked, and the activities that have been assigned to the user during disconnection. When reconnecting to the server, the runtime client discards all the information it has in its worklists and uses the one sent by the server. Before displaying the new worklist, it needs to update it to mark locked activities as such and to eliminate locked activities completed during disconnection. Note that the reconnections of the runtime client and the program execution client are done concurrently and, in most cases, the server will not yet be aware of the changes by the time the runtime client reconnects. This is the reason for keeping a list of locked activities and completed locked activities at the runtime client. Note that the list of completed activities is not discarded until the server notifies that the completion of these activities has been recorded in the database. Locked activities not executed during disconnection will remain locked.

Once the program execution client logs onto the server, it retrieves all the *activity terminated* messages from stable storage and sends them to the server. The server treats these messages as normal *activity terminated* messages, so it will send a message to the runtime client indicating that the results have been stored in the database. When such a message arrives, the runtime client can delete the corresponding entry from the list of completed locked activities. Depending on the mode of communication between the program execution client and the server, the *activity terminated* messages can be discarded immediately or after receiving an acknowledgement from the server. This affects the overall reliability but not the basic design, and since different systems implement this communication in different ways, we will not discuss this issue any further. Note that upon reconnection, the program execution client still keeps the information pertaining to locked activities that have not been executed since they still appear in the user worklist as being locked and may be invoked during a later disconnection. The program execution client discards information about locked activities only after storing the results of their execution in the database, via the server, or if the user *unlocks* the activity in the worklist.

4.5. Exception Handling

There are a number of issues that need special attention and have not been mentioned in the previous discussion. Most of them are related to exceptions and special cases and have no significant effect on the overall design. They are important, however, for the overall reliability and robustness of the system.

In FlowMark, activities have deadlines associated with them. If an activity has not been executed by the deadline, which is relative to the moment when the activity was assigned to one or more users, a notification mechanism is triggered. In general, the notification involves letting some user, presumably a supervisor, know that the activity has been delayed past its deadline and the most common response is to reassign the activity to some other user. In disconnected operation, an activity can be kept locked for a long period of time before it is actually executed. This is not a problem as long as the deadline does not expire, but if it does, the activity may belong to a user who is currently disconnected. There are several ways to deal with this problem. One is to assign the activity to a different user anyway and discard the results the first user may eventually produce. Another is to wait for the user to reconnect and then force the unlocking of the activity so it can be reassigned to another user. The solution or solutions adopted will depend on the importance of the activity.

A process instance involves several users. It is possible for one of these users, who has the necessary access rights, to delete the entire process while other users are working on it. If such is the case, then any results reported regarding that process are discarded and the clients are notified of the fact when they reconnect. There is an obvious loss of work in these scenarios but it is unavoidable. It is possible for activities to be running at the local site at the time the user wants to disconnect it from the server. Since these activities are known to the runtime client, and the disconnection operation is also processed by the runtime client, the system is able to detect these cases and delay the disconnection until there are no activities running at that site. We have opted for this solution, although there are other possibilities that may be more appropriate in other systems. For instance, the program execution client may be modified to remember it was executing these activities when it got disconnected and to treat them as a special case of locked activities.

Finally, before disconnecting, the program execution client should check whether the applications corresponding to the activities that have been locked are present. In FlowMark, there is no restriction on the nature of the activities included within a process as long as there is a way to trigger their execution. Note that they do not necessarily need to be computer programs. Phone calls, meeting and other human activities can be included as part of a process as long as there is an interface to trigger their occurrence and record their results upon termination. This can be easily accomplished through message and dialog windows displayed on a computer screen. However, this flexibility may create problems during disconnection, since it is possible to run a program on a machine different from the one in which the user is located. In those cases, unless some form of checking is done before disconnection, the user will realize that the supporting application is not locally available only when the activity is to be executed. The actual installation of supporting applications is left to the user, but the system will at least provide a mechanism whereby the user is notified of the problem before disconnecting.

5. Locating Clients in a Disconnected Environment

One of the most characteristic problems of mobile computing is to locate the mobile terminals and maintain accurate information about their location [16]. In our case, the problem is slightly different. We will rely on the underlying communication service to maintain the connection between a client and a server even if the client is located in a mobile computer. Moreover, connection always occurs at the client's request. The server never initiates a connection request or attempts to locate a given client. Although the users may get new activities assigned to them while disconnected, there is no notification service, i.e., the only way for a user to know about it is to connect to the system. This is also the case in current systems, where users need to actually log-in to know what has been assigned to them, but once online their worklist is dynamically maintained. To locate the clients, the approach taken is to force the clients to register with a server using a *system event* as opposed to just sending a message to that particular server. In this way, a client is free to reconnect with any server within the same system.

A more complex scenario arises when the client reconnects to a server in a different system, i.e., connected to another database. The server will not be able to perform any of the navigation steps corresponding to the processes in the worklist of the client simply because it uses a different database where this information has not been recorded. The approach taken is to introduce a server-to-server communication capability across FlowMark systems in such a way that if a server does not know about a particular activity, it will reroute the message to a server that knows about it [3]. Since the servers are located at predetermined sites, the only information needed is the name of the original database and its location. Such information is already included in the messages exchanged between the different components.

6. Discussion

Most of the ideas described in the previous section have been or are currently being implemented in a prototype that extends FlowMark functionality to support disconnected clients. The prototype has been implemented as an extension to the current version of FlowMark. In designing the prototype there were many tradeoffs to consider that will certainly have to be addressed in the design of any system of these characteristics. The basic question to answer is how much of the server and central database functionality is going to be duplicated at the clients. It is possible to go from almost none, as in current systems, to a fully replicated system in which each client is itself a server with access to a replicated database. Note that the more functionality is transferred to the clients, the more complex it becomes to maintain consistency between the different components. With FlowMark, there are some application scenarios that involve as many as 100,000 users. Even assuming they will share the clients, that still represents several thousand clients. There is an obvious limit to the overall size of the system for practical purposes and, therefore, there is a limit to the amount of functionality that can be incorporated into the clients while still maintaining the system within reasonable limits in terms of size and complexity, maybe not from the design point of view, since all clients are identical, but certainly from the user's point of view.

In this first prototype, we have chosen to incorporate only the basic functionality required to support disconnected clients as a proof of concept. Future work will involve exploring other possibilities.

The expected large scale of the system, prevents us from introducing changes to the server and database every time a new computing environments needs to be supported. Clients are logically the place where the particular characteristics of the computing environment should be considered. Thus, the current prototype does not include any changes to the core components of the system, these being the database, the server, and the buildtime client. The structure and semantics of a process are also left unchanged. Modifications are made to the runtime and program execution clients, which both simplifies the design and provides some degree of compatibility with existing FlowMark systems. This approach has the problem that the server does not understand the semantics of a locked activity. It is the clients who decide when an activity is locked and delayed in its execution. As part of future work, the notion of locked activity will be incorporated as one of the possible states of an activity, which will allow the server to recognize such a state and store the appropriate information in the database. This will alleviate some of the problems with deadline management when activities expire while locked. However, this will also require changes to the underlying data model and recompilation of existing processes to create new templates where activities are explicitly locked over the process model. In the long run, this will be necessary to take advantage of disconnected operation, but for the purposes of the prototype it was considered to be an orthogonal issue.

In the current prototype, the program execution client bears the burden of dealing with locked activities. While its basic functions are the same, much functionality has been added to cope with the demands of executing applications without access to the server. As explained above, the program execution client now has access to stable storage. The form of the stable storage is still being debated. Currently the file system is used, but it is conceivable that for some demanding applications the performance will be degraded unless a database is used. In the current version of FlowMark, both the runtime and the program execution client are memoryless and unable to survive failures. The addition of stable storage allows them not only to operate in disconnected mode but also to provide greater resilience to failures by relying on stable storage to avoid data loss. There are many trade-offs to consider, specially in the case of portable computers. A database can add significant overhead in terms of the footprint of the program execution client. On the other hand, if many activities are locked simultaneously, some form of indexing and organized data repository needs to be provided to guarantee fast access to the locked activities.

Finally, so far we have only considered the possibility of locking single activities once they are ready for execution. While useful, this is somewhat limited in its scope since the user is only able to work on activities not related in the partial order defined by the process. Most workflow systems make an activity visible to the users, i.e., eligible for execution, only when all previous activities to that one have successfully terminated. As part of future work we are considering the possibility of allowing users to lock groups of related activities. Note, however, that this implies duplicating much of the server's functionality at the clients and may also require to add new building blocks to the workflow model. To avoid excessive overhead, our current approach is to introduce *simple blocks*, a restricted set of activities that can all be assigned to a single user. Simple blocks may contain elementary activities or other simple blocks, but they cannot contain subprocesses. Given these restrictions, the only extentions needed on the client side are additional stable storage to store the definition of simple blocks, basic navigation functionality through a hierarchy of simple blocks, and standard features to manage data flow, e.g., for mapping of data containers. Access to (parts of) the database for role resolution and subprocess instantiation is not required. Thus, the overhead on the client side is fairly moderate.

7. Related Work

There is a considerable amount of research in workflow models and systems [10, 20, 26, 15, 9, 28, 30, 6]. However, both in research and in commercial systems, the issue of disconnected client support has not been fully addressed. Workflow systems like FlowMark, InConcert [24], and WorkFlo [7] assume users to be permanently connected to a more or less centralized workflow server while manipulating their worklists.

Recently, several proposals for distributed workflow management architectures have been made that address the issue of disconnected and unavailable clients. In Exotica/FMQM [1, 21] and in the architecture discussed for the INCAS, model [4], there is no central node that controls the execution of a workflow process. Workflow control and the current status of workflows are distributed across a number of processing nodes which are considered to be disconnected or unavailable quite frequently. Both systems use a reliable store and forward messaging mechanism to transfer activities to the next processing node, thereby avoiding the need for permanent connections. Hence, disconnections only result in delays in the sending of the messages.

Bussler [5] has recently proposed a system to support mobile clients in a workflow environment. This system requires the workflow designer to specify whether an activity can be executed in disconnected mode. It is based on the idea of downloading containers to the client, which ensures that the execution step is self contained. These containers also include the application to be invoked, that must be installed in the client by the WFMS before disconnection occurs.

In addition to the above research projects, there are currently more than 70 products that claim to be workflow solutions [8]. Many of these systems use store and forward messaging since they are based on workflow enabling tools like Lotus Notes or on e-mail. Some of them might claim that they support disconnected clients, however, they do not provide the full functionality of a real workflow system.

In more comprehensive systems like X-Workflow from Olivetti [25], a central mediator controls the control and data flow of a business process by distributing semi-structured e-mail messages to all users eligible to execute an activity. Once, a user selects an activity, an execution request is sent to the mediator which assigns the activity to the user and sends him/her the context data (input parameters) needed to execute the activity. Also, the mediator informs other users of this fact by sending a message which causes the intelligent mail system to remove the activity from the user's mail folder. In such environments, disconnected clients may still work on the last activity that they requested and received.

However, support for downloading a set of activities is not provided, although our approach could easily be adopted in this system.

8. Conclusions

We believe, along with [17], that there is considerable potential in combining mobile computing and workflow management systems. Until recently, little had been done to analyze and determine the impact of mobile computing on the design of workflow management systems. We have proposed a design for disconnected clients that is based on an existing workflow management system and that takes into account the collaborative aspects of the technology. While workflow systems are tools for cooperation, portable computers are generally viewed as tools for individual work. This is reflected in the architecture adopted by most workflow management systems that tends to be heavily centralized and requires the users to be connected to the central server. This paper has proposed a series of mechanisms to allow a workflow management system to support disconnected clients, effectively allowing users distributed over a wide geographic area and working with heterogeneous resources to cooperate, while preserving their mobility and independence.

One of the contributions of the paper is to point out the impact of disconnected clients on workflow management, which - to our knowledge - has been overlooked by previous research. In particular, we define the semantics of loading work to a mobile, disconnectable computer by introducing the notion of *locked activities* and the user's commitment to eventually execute them. Note that locked activities stay within the user's machine and that we allow the user to execute these activities even when the connection has been re-established. Therefore, locked activities also provide a way for users to select their preferred activities, remove them from the worklists of other users or to manually cache the workflow context for a number of activities at times of low network traffic. Finally, we prove the feasibility of our concept by providing an implementation based on FlowMark, a commercial workflow management system. Future work includes extending the mechanisms for loading blocks of related activities. This will help in migrating parts of a process instance from one FlowMark server to another. It can also be used to replicate process instances on a remote FlowMark server, thereby providing more flexibility for distributing the overall workload and to enhance fault-tolerance.

Acknowledgments

Part of this work was done while Gustavo Alonso, Roger Günthör, Divyakant Agrawal, Amr El Abbadi, and Mohan Kamath were visiting IBM Almaden Research Center. This work is partially supported by funds from IBM Hursley (Networking Software Division) and IBM Vienna (Software Solutions Division). Even though we refer to specific IBM products in this paper, no conclusions should be drawn about future IBM product plans based on this paper's contents. The opinions expressed here are our own.

References

1. G. Alonso, D. Agrawal, A. El Abbadi, C. Mohan, R. Günthör, and M. Kamath. Exotica/FMQM: A Persistent Message-Based Architecture for Distributed Workflow Management. In *IFIP WG8.1 Working Conference on Information System Development for Decentralised Organizations*, Trondheim, Norway, August 1995.
2. G. Alonso, R. Günthör, K. Kamath, D. Agrawal, A. El Abbadi, and C. Mohan. Exotica/FMDC: Handling Disconnected Clients in a Workflow Management System. In *Proceedings 3rd International Conference on Cooperative Information Systems*, Vienna, Austria, May 1995.
3. G. Alonso, M. Kamath, D. Agrawal, A. El Abbadi, R. Günthör, and C. Mohan. Failure Handling in Large Scale Workflow Management Systems. Research Report RJ 9913, IBM Almaden Research Center, November 1994.
4. D. Barbara, S. Mehrota, and M. Rusinkiewicz. INCAS: A Computation Model for Dynamic Workflows in Autonomous Distributed Environments. Technical report, Matsushita Information Technology Laboratory, April 1994.
5. Christoph Bussler. User Mobility in Workflow-Management-Systems. In *Proceedings of the Telecommunications Information Networking Conference (TINA '95)*, Melbourne, Australia, February 1995.
6. U. Dayal, M. Hsu, and R. Ladin. A Transaction Model for Long-running Activities. In *Proceedings of the Sixteenth International Conference on Very Large Databases*, pages 113–122, August 1991.
7. W. Fisher and J. Gilbert. FileNet: A Distributed System Supporting WorkFlo; a Flexible Office Procedures Control Language. In *IEEE Computer Society Office Automation Symposium*, pages 247–249, Gaithersburg, MD, April 1987.
8. C. Frye. Move to Workflow Provokes Business Process Scrutiny. *Software Magazine*, pages 77–89, April 1994.
9. Dimitrios Georgakopoulos, Mark F. Hornick, F. Manola, M.L. Brodie, S. Heiler, F. Nayeri, and B. Hurwitz. An Extended Transaction Environment for Workflows in Distributed Object Computing. *IEEE Computer Society Bulletin of the Technical Committee on Data Engineering*, 16(2):24–27, June 1993.
10. D. Georgakopoulos, M. Hornick, and A. Sheth. An Overview of Workflow Management: From Process Modeling to Workflow Automation Infrastructure. *Distributed and Parallel Databases*, 3(2):119–153, April 1995.
11. H. García-Molina, D. Gawlick, J. Klein, K. Kleissner, and K. Salem. Coordinating Multi-transaction Activities. In *Proceedings IEEE Spring Compcon*, 1991.
12. Y. Goldberg, M. Safran, and E. Shapiro. Active Mail - A Framework for Implementing Groupware. In *Proc. of the Conference on Computer-Supported Cooperative Work (CSCW)*, pages 281–288, Toronto, Canada, October 31 - November 4 1992.
13. M. Hammer and J. Champy. *Reengineering the Corporation: A Manifesto for Business Revolution*. Harper-Business, New York, 1993.
14. D. Hollinsworth. The workflow reference model. Technical Report TC00-1003, Workflow Management Coalition, December 1994.
15. M. Hsu. Special Issue on Workflow and Extended Transaction Systems. *Bulletin of the Technical Committee on Data Engineering, IEEE*, 16(2), June 1993.
16. T. Imielinsky and B.R. Badrinath. Querying in Highly Mobile Distributed Environments. In *Proceedings on the 18th VLDB Conference*, Vancouver, British Columbia, Canada, 1992.
17. Tomasz Imielinski and B. R. Badrinath. Mobile Wireless Computing: Solutions and Challenges in Data Management. *Communications of the ACM*, 37(10), October 1994.
18. IBM. *FlowMark - Managing Your Workflow, Version 2.1*. Document No. SH19-8243-00, March 1995.
19. IBM. *FlowMark - Modeling Workflow, Version 2.1*. Document No. SH19-8241-00, March 1995.
20. N. Krishnakumar and A. Sheth. Specifying Multi-system Workflow Applications in METEOR. Technical Report TM-24198, Bellcore, May 1994.
21. C. Mohan, G. Alonso, R. Günthör, and M. Kamath. Exotica: A research perspective on workflow management systems. *Bulletin of the Technical Committee on Data Engineering, IEEE*, 19(1), March 1995.
22. Workflow Management Coalition Members. Glossary, A Workflow Management Coalition Specification. Technical report, The Workflow Management Coalition, November 1994. Accessible via: http://www.aiai.ed.ac.uk/WfMC/.
23. T.W. Malone, K.R. Grant, K. Lai, R. Rao, and D. Rosenblitt. Semistructured Messages Are Surprisingly Useful for Computer-Supported Coordination. *ACM Transactions on Office Information Systems*, 5(2):115–131, 1987.

24. Dennis R. McCarthy and S. Sarin. Workflow and Transactions in InConcert. *IEEE Bulletin of the Technical Committee on Data Engineering*, 16(2):53–56, June 1993.

25. Olivetti Systems & Networks GmbH. *Ibisys X_Workflow-Vorgangssteuerung auf der Basis von X.400*, 1994. Produktbeschreibung.

26. A.P. Sheth. On Multi-system Applications and Transactional Workflows, Bellcore's projects PROMP and METEOR, 1994. Collection of papers and reports from Bellcore.

27. A. Sheth and M. Rusinkiewicz. On Transactional Workflows. *Bulletin of the Technical Committee on Data Engineering, IEEE*, 16(2), June 1993.

28. C. Tomlison, P. Attie, P. Cannata, G. Meredith, A. Sheth, M. Singh, and D. Woelk. Workflow Support in Carnot. *Bulletin of the Technical Committee on Data Engineering*, 16(2), June 1993. IEEE Computer Society.

29. D. Tsichritzis. Form Management. *Communications of the ACM*, 25(7):453–478, July 1982.

30. H. Waechter and A. Reuter. The ConTract Model. In A.K. Elmagarmid, editor, *Database Transaction Models for Advanced Applications*, chapter 7, pages 219–263. Morgan Kaufmann Publishers, San Mateo, 1992.

Distributed and Parallel Databases 4, 249–269 (1996)
© 1996 Kluwer Academic Publishers.

Supporting Mobile Database Access through Query by Icons

ANTONIO MASSARI   massari@infokit.dis.uniroma1.it
Dipart. di Informatica e Sistemistica, University of Rome "La Sapienza", 00198—Roma, Italy

SUSAN WEISSMAN   suew@cs.pitt.edu
PANOS K. CHRYSANTHIS   panos@cs.pitt.edu
Department of Computer Science, University of Pittsburgh, Pittsburgh, PA 15260, U.S.A.

Received May 9, 1995; Accepted February 12, 1996

Recommended by: Daniel Barbara, Ravi Jain and Narayanan Krishnakumar

Abstract.   In this paper, we present both the theoretical framework and a prototype of a query processing facility that supports the exploration and query of databases from a mobile computer through the manipulation of icons. Icons are particularly suitable for mobile computing since they can be manipulated without typing. The facility requires no special knowledge of the location or the content of the remote database nor understanding of the details of the database schema. Its iconic query language involves no path specification in composing a query. The query facility provides metaquery tools that assist in the formulation of complete queries in an incremental manner on the mobile computer and without involving access to the actual data in the remote database. By not requiring constant access and caching of the actual data, it is able to effectively cope with the inherent limitations in memory and battery life on the mobile computer, disconnections and restricted communication bandwidth, and the high monetary cost of wireless communication.

Keywords: mobile query processing, iconic query language, mobile computing, semantic distance, semantic and object model, path computations

1. Introduction

Advances in computer and wireless communication technologies have not only affected the way that we compute but, more significantly, they are changing the way we live and do business. For example, mobile users of a hospital paramedic unit arriving at an accident site need to easily access the medical history of the victims, regardless of the location and form of the information. They also need the capability of quickly locating and contacting medical personnel nearest to the accident site. That is, mobile users by means of hand-held computers equipped with a wireless interface, should be able (1) to compose a database query with minimum or no knowledge of how the database is structured and where it is located, and (2) to compose the query with a few key selections and minimum typing [3].

Motivated by these requirements, we present in this paper a query processing facility suitable for mobile database applications. The query processing facility, called *Query By Icons* (QBI), considers the inherent limitations in memory and battery power on the mobile computer, disconnections of the mobile computer for substantial periods, restricted communication bandwidth, and high monetary cost of wireless communication [4, 15].

The salient features of QBI are the following:

- An *iconic visual language* interface, which allows a user to compose a database query by manipulating icons using a pointing device like a light-pen on a hand-held pen-computer. Both structural information and constraints are visualized whereas the implicit ambiguity of iconic representation is resolved by automatically generated natural language.

- A *semantic data model* that captures locally within the mobile computer most of the aspects of the database structures while presenting the user with a set of simple representation structures. That is, a user is not required to have any special knowledge of the content of the underlying database nor the details of the database schema. A user perceives the whole database from any single focal object, as classes of objects expressed as *generalized attributes* of the focal object. Generalized attributes encapsulate and hide from the user the details of specifying a query.

- *Intensional* or *metaquery* tools that assist in the formulation of a complete query during disconnections. A query is formulated in an incremental manner without accessing actual data in the remote database to materialize intermediate steps. Data are accessed and transmitted back to the mobile computer *only* when a complete query is materialized.

While an iconic interface allows fast interactions (faster than typing) even when the user is moving, query formulation using intensional data offsets the expense and limitations of frequent wireless communication that is inherent to extensional browsing systems, e.g., [27, 29]. Metadata can be cached on the disk on the mobile computer since its definition changes rarely and its size is small compared to the actual database. Frequent communication results in slower response time due to the limited bandwidth of wireless links, as well as constant depletion of the computer's battery. Therefore, users can plan in advance to be disconnected from the network in order to save energy and reduce communication costs while actively exploring the database via intensional information on the mobile computer. In addition, users can continue with the formulation of their queries on the mobile computer even when the computer is accidentally disconnected.

In a mobile database environment, we envision QBI being used on both mobile and stationary hosts to query and explore a large distributed database managed by a number of servers on stationary hosts. In the next section, the conceptional model of QBI that defines the mobile user's perception of a database is discussed. Section 3 describes the components of a QBI prototype and illustrates its functionality through its use to query a medical database. QBI's theoretical framework is presented in Section 4 whereas the notion of *generalized attributes* which is central to QBI and its suitability as a query processing facility for mobile users is formally discussed in Section 5. Section 6 describes and evaluates three algorithms for generating generalized attributes on a mobile computer. The paper concludes with a discussion on related work in Section 7 and future work in Section 8.

2. QBI's conceptual data model

In QBI, the concepts of *class of objects* and *attribute of a class* exclusively form the external representation of the database structure due to their natural simplicity. Users are presented

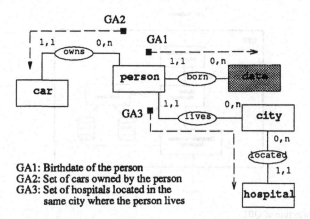

Figure 1.   Examples of generalized attributes.

with a database abstraction called *complete objects* [25], i.e., completely encapsulated objects, similar to the *universal relation* abstraction in relational databases [23]. Specifically, a user perceives the underlying database as a set of classes, each having several properties called *generalized attributes* (GA). In the same way that an attribute in the ER model [10] represents an elementary property of an entity, a GA expresses a *generic property* of a class.

Further, GAs encapsulate both *implicit* and *explicit* relationships among the objects within each focal object. That is, other object classes are viewed as GAs of the focal object. Thus, in QBI, each focal object provides a view of the whole underlying database from its own viewpoint. Let us illustrate the concept of GAs through an example. Assume the underlying database schema depicted in figure 1 using the Binary Graph Model [9, 25], which also forms QBI's theoretical framework (see Section 4). Here the rectangles denote object classes and ovals convey the interaction among classes.

A QBI user observes that the underlying database contains the same object classes shown in figure 1, namely, person, car, city, and hospital, but views the entire structure of the database by means of the GAs of any of these object classes. Of the three GAs of the class person shown in figure 1, consider attribute GA3 whose value is a subset of the object class hospital. By observing GA3, the user perceives that a hospital is located in a city and is an attribute of person. A generalized attribute with similar meaning exists from the viewpoint of hospital. That is, from the view of a hospital object class, this GA is a subset of persons corresponding to, "All the people living in the same city where the hospital is located". Also, the same information, could be obtained by observing the GAs of city.

3.   QBI prototype

In this section, we will describe our QBI prototype and how it can be used to query a Medical Database that includes radiological data from a mobile computer.

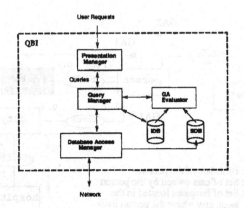

Figure 2. The architecture of QBI.

The QBI prototype is written in C for the MS-Windows environment using the toolkit XVT, and is currently running on NCR System 3125 Pen-top computers with PenDOS and MS-Windows for Pen Computing. The size of the QBI prototype itself is only 0.5 MBytes whereas it stores less than 100 KBytes of intensional information about the radiological medical database.

The overall architecture of the QBI prototype is diagrammed in figure 2 and consists of four modules: The *Presentation Manager* which is responsible for all interactions with the user; the *Query Manager* which supports the specification of queries; the *GA Evaluator* which computes the generalized attributes; and the *Database Access Manager* which is responsible for any remote access to the actual data in the database on a stationary host, as well as managing the sporadic updates to the metadata and statistics about the underlying database. GAs are computed on demand because, given an object class, there is potentially an infinite number of GAs associated with an object class and only a small fraction of them is useful in the construction of a particular query.

The execution of the presentation manager as well as of the query manager and the GA evaluator, is supported by two databases, namely, the *Intensional Database* (IDB) and the *Statistical Database* (SDB). The IDB contains all the metadata and the visual data for the iconic representation. Whereas the SDB contains statistical information on the instances in the database used for the evaluation of the GAs.

3.1. QBI's iconic visual language interface

The presentation manager structures the interactions with a user around three windows, each dedicated to a specific aspect in the specifications of a query. The three windows composing the QBI interface are referred to as the *Workspace Window*, the *Query Window* and the *Browser Window*.

3.1.1. Workspace Window.
When the QBI application starts, the user is asked to select the database to be considered for querying, in our example a radiological database. In

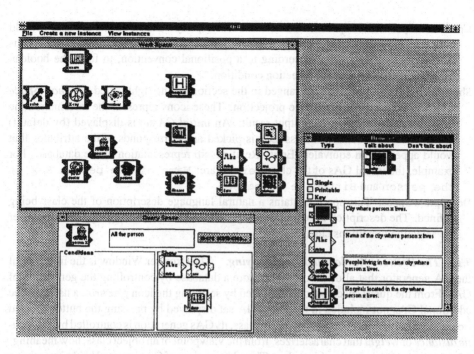

Figure 3. The QBI interface.

response, the Workspace window appears and displays a set of *icons* corresponding to both *primitive* classes that are actually stored in the database and *derived* classes representing stored queries (see figure 3).

Every icon has an *image* conveying a metaphorical meaning for the class. Below the image is a *label* that allows for easy identification. A full natural language sentence *description* is also provided that can be read by pointing at the icon. This description is automatically generated based on the method described in [8] and is essential for disambiguating the meaning between various icons. Even the *shape* of the icon conveys information. When forming a query, icons representing compatible object classes that are allowed to be combined in a selection condition of a query are associated with a specific geometric outline, similar to a jigsaw puzzle piece. The shape of an icon can appear flat, such as the patient icon, or as a *stack* of shapes, such as the hospital icon found at the bottom of the Browser Window in figure 3. This stacked representation tells the user how many instances of the object class can be referred to with this one icon. The hospital icon appears stacked since it represents a group of hospitals.

3.1.2. Query Space Window.

Pointing at an icon in the Workspace corresponds to selecting its object class for a query via the activation of the Query Space. If the class icon for person is picked from the Workspace, the Query Space shown at the bottom left of figure 3 will become visible to the user. There are several parts to this window that allow a user to compose a query based on the *select-project paradigm*:

Conditions Space: This space on the left side of the query window allows the user to build both GAs constituting the atoms of a selection condition and the condition itself. Atoms can be combined together, according to a positional convention, to form the boolean expression representing the selection condition.

Show Space: Icons can also be arranged in the section on the right called the *Show Space* which is used for specifying the projection. These icons represent the information the user chooses to view in the output result. An *initial GA set* is displayed (by default) in the Show Space when a class icon is picked and corresponds to the attributes that would appear in an equivalent Entity Relationship representation of the database. For example, the initial GAs of the class person are: Name of the person, Sex of the person and Birthdate of person.

Description Space: This space contains a natural language description of the class being defined. The description is automatically generated and dynamically updated whenever the selection conditions change.

3.1.3. The Browser Window and metaquerying.

The Browser Window is the interface of the GA generator that allows a user to explore a database by controlling the generation of GAs. From the query space window activated by selecting the icon person, a user can see additional GAs not included in the initial GA set displayed by pressing the button labeled more attributes. With a given object class, its GAs generation is controlled by a *semantic distance* or *weight* that characterizes, from the viewpoint of an object class, how meaningful a particular GA is for the object class. The additional set of GAs is sorted by their semantic distance so that the most meaningful GAs are shown first. Thus, by observing the top of the list of GAs the user can have an immediate perception of the most meaningful attributes of person. The Browser window of figure 3 shows the additional GA city where person X lives. Additional GAs such as this one can then be dragged from the Browser window into the Conditions and Show spaces within the Query window when forming a query.

To empower the user with the ability to control his/her view of the database environment, a set of *metaquery tools* are provided within the Browser. These *metaquery operators* permit the specification of filter conditions on the GA set. Hence, a user interested in very distant properties of the class person can easily explore these properties, by restricting the search of the desired GAs within a smaller GA set. For example, one useful metaquery operator is used when a user desires GAs which are associated with a specific object class. If the user is interested in all the GAs that *talk about* city, the icon for city from the Workspace window can be moved into the **Talk about** space of the Browser (see figure 3). In particular it is possible to express the following metaquery conditions: (1) *single, printable, or key* selects only single valued, printable GAs, or key GAs used to identify an instance of a class, respectively, (2) *type* selects all the GAs that represent a subset of a particular object class and, (3) *talk about, don't talk about* selects GAs that are associated or not associated with a specified class. All the metaquery conditions are combined in a conjunctive expression by default.

3.2. Query examples

Let us revisit the hospital paramedic unit example mentioned in the introduction. As a patient is rushed to the most appropriate hospital, a specialist living within close proximity of the hospital is notified. For this type of information, we need to determine the set of doctors living in the same city in which they work. The result of this query is a subset of the class doctor that can be saved as a *derived class*. In order to build the derived class it is necessary to specify the selection condition *Cond*: *The city where the doctor works is equal to the city where the doctor lives*. *Cond* can be specified by connecting the two GAs: City where doctor x lives and City where doctor x works with the connective Is equal to.

The first GA is immediately found by scrolling the list in the Browser window. This GA is dragged by the user from the Browser window into the condition space of the Query window. As far as the second GA is concerned, the user needs to perform a metaquery on the GA set of doctor by dragging the icon city into the **Type** space of the Browser window. The first GA shown in the list represents the "best" connection between doctor and city and it coincides with the GA the user was looking for, that is: *City where a hospital is located. Such a hospital is the hospital where doctor x works.*

The second GA is then dragged into the condition space and the two GAs are "attached" together; since they have the same type (that of city), their shapes allow this operation to be performed. Once the two GAs have been attached together, a dialogue box containing a set of valid connectives appears. By choosing the equality connective the user ends the selection part of her/his query. In the description space a sentence explaining the selection query is automatically added (figure 4). For the projection, the user does not have to pick the name, sex and birthdate of the doctor because they are part of the initial GA set of doctor and must be already in the Show space. In order to know in which city the hospital and

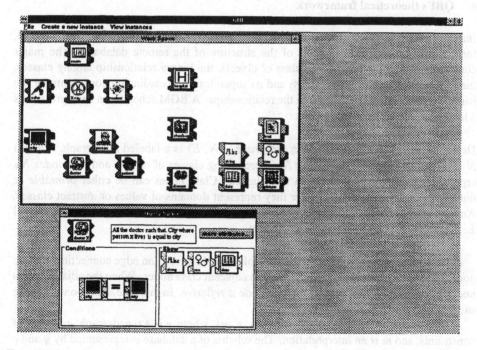

Figure 4. A query.

doctor are located, the user simply drags the appropriate, i.e., city, icon from the Browser into the Show space.

The result of a query constitutes a derived class of the picked class and as such it can be stored in the intensional database. In the above example, after the user chooses a label, say Lucky Drs, for the newly created derived class, the new class is assigned an icon which becomes part of the icon set contained in the workspace window and can be used as if it were a primitive one. The image of this icon will be that of a doctor since this GA is a subset of the object class doctor. To materialize this query, all the user has to do is drag this new icon to a special system icon called the "printer". This operation corresponds to forwarding the corresponding query to the remote database, requesting for its execution, and fetching the query result for display.

As seen with this example, QBI is very useful in a mobile computing environment as queries require very little typing. Also, only a small screen is required since queries do not require any form of path specification. The underlying, formal schema is hidden and feedback in the form of natural language and shapes is very helpful for users with a limited knowledge of database languages. In addition, intensional data and metaquery tools are provided to users to allow them to formulate queries even when the computer is disconnected. In the following section, we will formally define the semantic data model used by QBI, as well as the concepts of generalized attributes and semantic distance. In further sections, we will show how the internal algorithms for GA generation were improved for a mobile environment.

4. QBI's theoretical framework

Internally, QBI uses the Binary Graph Model (BGM) [9, 25], a semantic data model, for capturing most of the aspects of the structure of the remote database. The major constructs of this model are: the class of objects, the binary relationship among classes, the ISA relationship between a class and its superclass, and cardinality constraints for the participation of class instances into the relationships. A BGM schema can be expressed as a labeled graph called *typed-graph*.

Definition 4.1 (Typed graph). A *typed-graph* $g(N, E)$ is a labeled multigraph. The set N of nodes consists of *class nodes* N_C representing classes of objects and *role nodes* N_R representing relationships between two classes. Class nodes can be either *printable* or *nonprintable* depending on whether they represent domains of values or abstract classes. An edge in E can only link a class node to a role node and is associated with a unique label L. Each role node has a degree equal to two.

A class node is said to be *adjacent* to a role node if there is an edge connecting the two nodes. Each role node will have exactly two adjacent class nodes. When the adjacent class nodes are coincident we say that the role node is *reflexive*. In this case, labels on edges are useful for disambiguating the two edges.

A BGM database is defined as a triple $\langle g, c, m \rangle$, where g is a typed-graph, c is a set of constraints, and m is an interpretation. The schema of a database is represented by g and c whereas an instance of a database (extension) are represented by the notion of interpretation.

Definition 4.2 (Interpretation). Let g be a typed-graph. An *interpretation* for g is a function m mapping each class node $n_c \in N_C$ to a set $m(n_c)$ of objects and each role node $n_r \in N_R$ to a set $m(n_r)$ of pairs $\langle lbl_1(n_r): x_1, lbl_2(n_r): x_2 \rangle$, where lbl_1, lbl_2 are functions returning the labels of the two edges connected to n_r ($lbl_1, lbl_2: N_R \rightarrow L$) and $\langle x_1, x_2 \rangle \in m(n_{c1}) \times m(n_{c2})$ where n_{c1} and n_{c2} are the adjacent class node of n_r.

That is, an interpretation specifies the valid combinations of values from the underlying classes. The set of constraints on the database referred to in this paper are the minimum (ATLEAST) and maximum (ATMOST) cardinality constraints, and the subclass-superclass relationship constraint (ISA).

Definition 4.3 (Constraints). The set c contains: (1) ATLEAST(k, n_{c1}, n_r) specifies that an instance of class node n_{c1} can participate in at least k interpretations involving the adjacent role node n_r; (2) ATMOST(k, n_{c1}, n_r) specifies that an instance of class node n_{c1} can participate in at most k interpretations involving the adjacent role node n_r; (3) ISA$(n_{\hat{c}}, n_c)$ specifies that the class $n_{\hat{c}}$ is a subset of the class n_c (i.e., $m(n_{\hat{c}}) \subseteq m(n_c)$). The role nodes connected to n_c are considered as also being connected to $n_{\hat{c}}$, i.e., $n_{\hat{c}}$ *inherits* the edges of n_c.

Currently, we assume single inheritance, hence each class node has to belong to one and only one *class hierarchy*. In order to facilitate type checking of query expressions, we define the notion of *type* of a class as a class hierarchy. That is, the class nodes belonging to a class hierarchy have the same type. Note that if n_{c1} and n_{c2} have different types, their interpretations are disjoint.

Figure 5 shows an example of a typed graph which is a fragment of the medical database used in the previous section. The rectangular boxes represent class nodes (the printable ones are grayed) while the ovals represent role nodes. No label on an edge is shown since there are no reflexive role nodes that need to be disambiguated. The annotations (m, n) on edges represent (ATLEAST, ATMOST) cardinality constraints. ISA constraints are denoted by a thick arrow from a subclass node to its superclass.

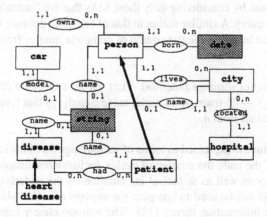

Figure 5. A typed graph.

5. Generalized attributes

As mentioned above, the concept of GA in QBI represents the way in which a user perceives the relationships among objects. Internally, a GA is strictly related to the concept of *path* in a typed-graph capturing the database schema, where a path is a sequence of adjacent class and role nodes always starting and ending with a class node.

Definition 5.1 (Path). Let $\mathcal{G}$ be a typed-graph. A *step s* on $\mathcal{G}$ is the triple $\langle class_1(s), role(s), class_2(s)\rangle$ where $class_1(s) = n_{c1}$, $class_2(s) = n_{c2} \in N_C$ are adjacent to $role(s) = n_r \in N_R$. A *path p* on $\mathcal{G}$ is the sequence $s_1, s_2, \ldots, sk$ of steps on $\mathcal{G}$ such that, for $i = 1, 2, \ldots, k-1$, $class_2(s_i) = class_1(s_{i+1})$. The first and the last class node of a path p, i.e., $class_1(s_1(p))$ and $class_2(s_{length(p)}(p))$, will be denoted with *first(p)* and *last(p)* respectively.

Given two class nodes n_c (*picked class node*) and $n_{\hat{c}}$, a path p starting in n_c and ending in $n_{\hat{c}}$ defines a GA of n_c as a function mapping each instance x of n_c onto a set of instances of $n_{\hat{c}}$.

Definition 5.2 (Generalized attribute). Let $\mathcal{G}$ be a typed-graph, n_c a class node of $\mathcal{G}$ and p a path on $\mathcal{G}$ such that $first(p) = n_c$; the GA of the class node n_c associated to p is a function $\gamma_p\colon m(first(p)) \to \wp(m(last(p)))$ mapping every object $x_0 \in m(n_c)$ to a subset of objects of the last class node of p, $m(last(p))$.

A GA can be either *single valued* or *multivalued* depending on the cardinality constraints of the role nodes involved in the path. Since a GA is a function γ_p returning a set of objects belonging to $m(last(p))$ we will say that γ_p has a *type* that is the type of *last(p)*.

A path in a typed-graph can be cyclic. Cyclic paths are allowed since they can represent useful properties, e.g., People living in the same city where the person lives. As a consequence the set of possible GAs associated with a class node is infinite. Since not all paths are equally meaningful, and in order to cope with infinitely long (cyclic) paths, QBI defines a *semantic distance function* on paths which returns a value for each path representing the meaningfulness of the corresponding GA. A finite set of GAs of an object is constructed by considering only those GAs that are "meaningful enough" for the specification of a query. A similar notion to that of semantic distance function in QBI is the notion of semantic length in the generation of complete queries from incomplete path expressions [17].

Definition 5.3 (Semantics distance function). Let γ_p be a GA of a class node n_c. The function Semd: $\Gamma(n_c) \to \Re$ maps γ_p to a real value $\text{Semd}(\gamma_p)$ that represents how much γ_p is semantically distant from n_c.

The semantic distance is expressed in terms of various aspects of the structure of the GA such as the length of the path, the number of cycles, inclusion/exclusion of specific paths, cardinality constraints as well as statistical information on the underlying database. The statistical information can be used to compute the *entropy* of a GA which is the measure of uncertainty in the information theory [13]. The entropy clearly captures the fact that a user considers a GA only if the GA conveys some information. By taking entropy into consideration, a large number of less meaningful GAs, such as "all the persons that have a name equal to the model name of a car", can be discarded.

Given a semantic distance function *Semd* and a *threshold* value $\tau \in \Re$, the finite GA set of n_c, with respect to Semd, will be determined by:

$$\bar{\Gamma}_{\text{Semd}}(n_c) = \{\gamma_p \in \Gamma(n_c) \mid \text{Semd}(\gamma_p) < \tau\}$$

provided that Semd is monotonically increasing.

The following function was implemented in the QBI prototype to compute the semantic distance of a new GA $\gamma_{p'}$ resulting from adding a new step to an existing GA γ_p. Let the new step being added to γ_p be $e = \langle u, v, w \rangle$ (i.e., $p' = p \cup e$).

$$\begin{aligned}
\text{Semd}\gamma_{p'} = {} & (c_1 * \text{length}(p')) + (c_2 * \text{num\_cycles}(p') \\
& + (c_3 * \text{max\_cardinality}(p) * \text{atmost\_cardinality}(e) - 1) + \text{NPW} * c_4 \\
& + \mathcal{E} * (c_5/\text{avg\_cardinality}(p') - c_5) + \text{NPU} * c_6
\end{aligned}$$

where NPW, NPU and $\mathcal{E}$ are binary flags with 0 or 1 value, and c_1, c_2, c_3, c_4, c_5 and c_6 are positive real constants used as semantic penalties for properties that may exist in a new GA path. As a GA's path becomes longer (length(p') or cyclic (num_cycles(p')), or its cardinality dramatically increases (max_cardinality(p) * atmost_cardinality(e)), so does the semantic distance associated with this GA. The length is defined to be the number of role nodes connectors used by the path and does not include any class-superclass connectors (i.e., "is a" connectors).

A path that ends with a class node w which is *not* printable, represents a relationship between n_c and another abstract object class. This object class will contain simple attributes that have not been discovered. However, because there is no information for the user that is directly obtainable from this path, the path is penalized by assigning NPW to 1. Otherwise NPW is 0.

In the QBI prototype, the current weight increase c_6 for going through printable nodes is 300 and is equivalent to the penalty c_2 associated with a class node being a member of a cycle. The other penalty constants are $c_1 = 200$, $c_3 = 0.02$, $c_4 = 20$ and $c_5 = 100$. All penalty constants have be adjusted for better performance after a series of experiments while making sure that the Semd remains monotonically increasing.

6. Mobile GA generation

In a mobile environment, QBI's method of query formulation and use of intensional data limits the cost of frequent wireless communication with respect to the materialization of complete queries. Visualization of the database as well as cost effective query formulation is done primarily through the manipulation of generalized attributes. As stated above, a GA γ_p is simply a path p in a typed-graph $\mathcal{G}$. Every time a step is added to an existing GA path, a new GA is formed and its associated (real number) semantic distance value (sd-value) is computed by the function Semdγ_p. The generation of GAs is an instance of a *path computation* [2, 16], and is clearly the most computationally expensive part of

QBI. The cost of the semantic distance function depends on its complexity which, in turn, is a measure of its accuracy to express the meaningfulness of a GA. However, this cost is independent of the environment in which QBI is executing. On the other hand, the value for the threshold that terminates the generation of GAs can be tuned to consider the capabilities of the system. In the case of the mobile computer, the threshold τ is defined as a function of the available memory, the energy level and the response time:

$$\tau = C_1(\text{free\_memory}) + C_2(\text{energy\_level}) + C_3(\text{cpu\_speed})$$
$$+ C_4(\text{resp\_requirements})$$

where C_i are user defined parameters. Given that the first two parameters, free_memory and energy_level, vary over time, the threshold τ dynamically changes as well.

The initial GA evaluator in our QBI prototype traverses the typed-graph in a *depth-first search* (DFS) manner. Although this is also the approach traditionally used in path computations [2, 16], it has turned out to be unsuitable for mobile operations. First, since it does not generate GAs sorted based on their sd-value, an additional sorting phase is required for the presentation. More importantly, the DFS strategy is not compatible with a dynamically defined threshold. DFS allows for the possibility of a dynamically set threshold to terminate the execution of the GA evaluator before the generation of GAs associated with a low sd-value and after spending a significant amount of time in generating GAs with higher sd-values. For these reasons, we have explored two other alternatives, the *best-first search* (BEST) and *breadth-first search* (BFS) based GA evaluators.

The BEST algorithm explores the given graph $\mathcal{G}$ by maintaining an order among the GAs found based on the semantic distances associated with the GAs. At each iteration, BEST always considers the GA with the minimal semantic value. The BEST-based algorithm uses: (1) a sorted List to maintain an order among the GAs produced, (2) (n_c), the starting class node chosen by the user, (3) a path p associated with every GA γ_p and a total semantic distance $\text{Semd}(\gamma_p)$, and (4) the function weight (u, w), which computes the distance between two class nodes u and w, where $\mathcal{G}$ is the given typed-graph and for each step $e \in \mathcal{G}, e = \langle u, v, w \rangle$. Below are shown the basic steps for the algorithm.

BEST $(\omega = n_c, \gamma_p, \tau, \Gamma(n_c))$
_____
Do
    For each step $e = \langle u, v, w \rangle$ where $u = \omega$
        Mark every class node in p of γ_p as newly visited in order to detect cycles.
        Calculate $\text{Semd}(\gamma_{p'}) = \text{Semd}(\gamma_p) + \text{weight}(u, w)$
        If $(\text{Semd}(\gamma_{p'})) \leq \tau$ Then
                $p' = p \cup e$
                Sorted_Insert(List, $\gamma_{p'}$, p', $\text{Semd}(\gamma_{p'})$)
    End For
    If the List is not empty
        $\gamma_p = \text{First\_Of\_List}(\text{List})$
        $\omega = last(p)$ (the p associated with our new γ_p)
        $\Gamma(n_c) = \Gamma(n_c) \cup \gamma_p$
While the List is *not* empty

The BFS algorithm, the second alternative GA evaluator, explores the given typed-graph $\mathcal{G}$ in a level-by-level fashion. Only when all the class nodes at a given level are explored does the algorithm move on to the next level. All of the items used by BEST are also used by BFS, except that maintaining an order among the GA paths that are to be expanded is now done by a Queue instead of a List.

In accordance to the basic BFS algorithm, the Queue was sorted every time all the class nodes at a level x were explored. Although, sorting would be performed more often, a very small number of GAs would be sorted each time, and BEST's incremental sort with many comparisons would be avoided. However, it has turned out that this is not enough, since there are *no* order guarantees among the weights of GAs ending at different levels along different paths. Because of the binary flags NPW, NPU, and $\mathcal{E}$ whose values are dependent on the type of the class node, all paths produced by p that end at level x are *not* guaranteed to have smaller sd-values than all paths found at level $x + 1$. Hence, BFS requires an explicit sorting phase as DFS.

6.1. Advantages and disadvantages of DFS, BFS, and BEST

With BEST and BFS, the main advantage over DFS is efficiency in finding meaningful GAs. BEST generates GAs in the order of their meaningfulness to the user based on their semantic distance from the focal object class n_c. With BFS, GAs with the shortest paths are generated first, and it is highly likely that these paths are very semantically meaningful from the viewpoint of n_c due to the monotonically increasing property of Semd along a path. The ordering performed by BEST and BFS is useful in a mobile environment since the semantic distance threshold τ could be set by a function that describes the limitations of the mobile unit. With BEST, only the most meaningful GAs with respect to these limitations would be generated, and it does not require a separate explicit sorting phase.

However, unlike DFS, both BEST and BFS maintain complex data structures in the form of a sorted List or Queue. In the worst case, each element added to the List must be compared to all the other elements before finding its correct location. If the graph is very dense, with each node ω having a large degree, the number of comparisons will be very high. An additional indexing structure could be used to combat the cost of insertion. This approach, however, would require more space. One advantage BFS has in this regard is that it does not need to perform an expensive incremental sorting on each insertion of a new GA the way BEST does.

In addition, adding a step $e = \langle u, v, w \rangle$ to an existing path p may cause the ending class node w to become a member of a cycle. Detection of this in DFS only requires a marker associated with the node w. If the class node w is already a part of the path p before the addition of e, then the node will be marked. Hence, another factor that increases the execution time of BEST and BFS when compared to DFS, is the method needed for cycle detection. In order to detect if the node w is part of a cycle, all the class nodes of the path p currently being expanded must be marked. This prevents the detection of a false cycle whenever two separate routes from the focal point object n_c are being expanded concurrently and both reach the same node. However, the cost for this is one traversal of the path p every time a step is added. Since each of these algorithms have comparable advantages and disadvantages, further investigation is necessary in order to determine which one is the most useful with respect to a mobile computing environment.

6.2. Evaluating the GA generation methods

To the user, the two most important criteria are *response-time* and *quality* of GAs i.e., the semantic distances of the GAs produced. These are two important criteria in determining how well each of the algorithms proposed for the GA evaluator perform. However, within a mobile environment, the GA evaluator should operate without depleting a large amount of the mobile unit's resources. The method proposed above for controlling the amount of resources used by the GA evaluator is the notion of a dynamically changing threshold τ. How effectively a changing threshold performs with respect to finding meaningful attributes and response-time must be evaluated.

Two tests were done in order to evaluate the three GA Generation Methods discussed in the previous sections. The first test compares the three algorithms with regards to the quality of attributes found by each. The second test evaluates the three implementations under a dynamically changing threshold. These experiments were done using an Intel 486DX, 66 MHz PC with 16 MBytes RAM.

Test 1: Meaningful attribute test (MAT)

Task: Each algorithm was given the task of finding a given number (X) of GAs for the `doctor` object class in the radiological database of the QBI prototype.

Parameters: The semantic weight threshold *remained* a constant 1800. At this value, the system produced a sorted attribute list (SAL) of 947 GAs. For each successive test run, the number of GAs required (X) was *increased* by 100.

Each algorithm was timed from the moment it was invoked until it was able to produce a sorted list of the required number (X) of attributes. In addition, to measure the quality of the attributes produced by the algorithm, a comparison was made to see how many of the attributes produced by the algorithm matched the first X attributes found in SAL. Figure 6 is a graph of these test runs.

Test 2: Dynamic threshold test (DTT)

Task: Each algorithm was required to find all the GAs below a given semantic distance threshold τ for the `doctor` object class in the radiological database of the QBI proto-type.

Parameters: The semantic distance threshold τ was changed for each successive test run. It was incremented by a value of 100 for each run.

Each algorithm was timed from the moment it was invoked until it was able to produce a sorted list of attributes below the given semantic distance threshold. Figure 7 is a graph that

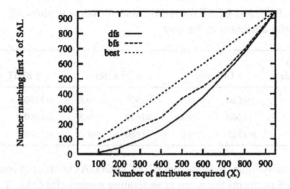

Figure 6. MAT: Quality of attributes found.

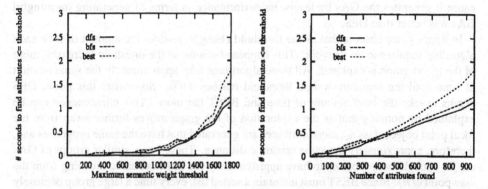

Figure 7. DTT: Time to find attributes below a given   *Figure 8.* DTT: Number of attributes found below a
threshold value.   given threshold.

shows how many seconds it took each algorithm to find all the GAs below a given thresh-
old τ. For each threshold τ, a certain number of attributes in the typed-graph $\mathcal{G}$ will have
distances below τ. In order to compare the results of MAT with this test, another graph
shown in figure 8 was created. In this graph, the amount of time required by each algorithm is mapped to the number of attributes within $\mathcal{G}$ that are below the corresponding
threshold.

6.2.1. Implications of MAT and DTT.

Suppose that in a mobile application users would
be able to obtain all the information they wanted if the Browser Window always displayed
the first 450 most meaningful attributes for the doctor object class. Figure 6 shows that
BFS finds the top 450 most meaningful attributes by generating a total of 600 attributes
from the typed-graph $\mathcal{G}$. From figure 7, it is apparent that BFS finds these 600 attributes
within 0.72 seconds. Also, from figure 8, finding 600 attributes within 0.72 seconds using
BFS corresponds to a threshold of $\tau = 1600$. Of course, these figures could have been
calculated using any of the three implementations. Below is a table that corresponds to the

answers for DFS, BFS, and BEST for the Browser Window to show 400, 600, and 800 of
the most meaningful attributes to the user.

Number attributes	τ DFS sec.		τ BFS sec.		τ BEST sec.	
400	≈1620	≈.7	≈1500	≈.6	≈1390	≈.42
600	≈1640	≈.8	≈1630	≈.8	≈1590	≈.85
800	≈1725	≈1.0	≈1680	≈1.0	≈1660	≈1.3

MAT and especially figure 6, show that BEST finds GAs in order of increasing semantic
distance while DFS performs the worst at generating meaningful GAs. This result was expected since BEST does not require an additional explicit sorting phase. BFS's performance
was between DFS and BEST. The algorithm does require an explicit sorting phase, but because it generates the GAs by levels, its performance in terms of generating meaningful
GAs was better than DFS.

In figure 7, we observe that as the threshold changes, so does the amount of time each
algorithm requires to do its work. This happens because as the threshold increases, more
of the typed-graph is explored. All three algorithms take approximately the same amount
of time until the semantic weight threshold reaches 1400. Soon after this point, DFS
begins to take the least amount of time and BEST the most. This phenomenon can be
explained by noticing that as the exploration of the graph moves further away from the
focal point object class n_c, more attributes are generated that have the same properties and,
therefore, approximately the same semantic distance. These large, similar groups of GAs
are far enough away from n_c to have approximately the same semantic meaning from the
viewpoint of n_c. Since BEST must maintain a sorted list, every time a large group of closely
weighted GAs are produced, they must be placed in their proper position in the list. This
requires a large number of traversals and accounts for the decrease in BEST's performance
as the threshold τ increases.

6.2.2. An integrated mobile GA evaluator.
Within a mobile environment, the mobile
computer could set the semantic distance threshold by a function depending on how much
memory, processing, battery power, and delay the host and user can afford. Therefore,
the mobile computer would be trying to reserve its resources and not waste time or energy
finding GAs that are of little value to the user. BEST can generate the most meaningful GAs
with respect to these limitations. Although the BEST algorithm is more compatible with a
mobile environment, its response-time suffers as the threshold is dynamically increased.

Although our original intention was to replace the currently used DFS algorithm in QBI
with either the BEST or BFS algorithms, our experimentation clearly showed that one algorithm does not meet all the needs of a mobile GA evaluator. Therefore, we propose to
combine these techniques into one integrated mobile GA evaluator. Since each algorithm
only requires a few kilobytes, this proposed integrated evaluator will not require a dramatic
increase in the amount of code kept on the mobile computer. BEST will be the default
algorithm of the mobile GA evaluator, since it does produce a sorted list of GAs. In a mobile environment, as long as a low semantic threshold τ is computed, the BEST algorithm

will be used. However, as the limitations of the mobile host are relaxed, the GA evaluator will switch to a BFS that can facilitate a broader, sweeping search of the graph with a better response-time. Finally, whenever there are few restrictions on the mobile host (e.g., when the mobile host is stationary and attached to docking mobility-support station), or the user wants to examine a large number of GAs, a switch to a "focus" DFS algorithm would facilitate the exploration of the database using more resources. Therefore, GA evaluator thresholds can be set in much the same way that the ER threshold was set for the query window (see Subsection 3.12). As τ changes dynamically and captures the status of the mobile host, the search technique used by the GA evaluator will also change to accommodate these limitations. We are currently investigating this integrated mobile GA evaluator.

7. Related work

Most of the work related to our approach has been done in the areas of database graphical user interfaces, and data modeling.

In the area of graphical user interfaces a large amount of research has been produced with the purpose of facilitating user interaction while still maintaining the highly expressive power of the query language [7, 20]. Most of the proposed systems adopt form, tabular, or diagram based visual paradigms. Early examples of these types of visual query languages that use a *relational external data model* are QBE [35] and G+ [11]. In QBE, the query is made by filling in templates of relations. Users do not need to remember attribute names or variable names. Queries are specified by typing example tuples expressing the information that is being requested. G+ makes use of a diagrammatic paradigm by using a graph whose edges correspond to the tuples in a relation.

Semantic data models go even further than the relational model in terms of providing the user with a more abstract logical view of the data. Of these, the ER model [10] is often used as the external data model in existing visual query systems. GORDAS [12], QBD* [5], GRAQULA [28, 33], and GQL/ER [34] are examples of graphical visual query systems that provide the user with an ER diagram of the schema. Queries in these systems are formulated by drawing nodes and edges to be matched in the schema diagram. That is, queries are specified as subgraphs of the ER schema diagram with certain nodes and edges replicated as necessary. Selection conditions and projections are specified as annotations of the nodes and edges. For example, in GORDAS and QBD*, once a user selects the entities and relationships of interest, a simplified hierarchical diagram of the schema is provided in order to aid in the formulation of queries. In general, the difference between these systems is their varying support in the specification of aggregation, quantification, and recursion. Further, GQL/ER combines features of the universal relational model and the ER model without the support of aggregation or quantification. PICASSO [19], on the other hand, provides an external universal relation data model that interfaces a universal relational database system. In PICASSO, maximal objects are represented as hyperedges in a hypergraph which contains textual attribute labels. Queries are formulated via mouse clicks which reveal pop-up menus that allow for the selection of aggregate and set operators as well as comparison operators used in predicate formulation. Adding a hyperedge with the mouse creates a tuple variable and, therefore, no character-type tuple variables are necessary. Another visual query system which as QBI is based on a richer semantic model than the ER model and universal relational model is Ski [21]. In Ski, by means of a set of semantics operators, users can dynamically construct portions of the database schema and peruse the schema for related information, having complete access to an underlying semantic data language. Similar to QBI, this perusal is not performed navigationally but semantically. As opposed to QBI, Ski is diagram based and supports navigation through the paths of the underlying database schema.

Compared to diagrammatic visual languages, the ease and effectiveness of QBI with respect to unsophisticated users was established through an empirical evaluation of QBI and QBD* [24, 6]. In this study users were classified into unskilled users with little, if any, training in databases, and skilled ones. The two performance measures used were the time in seconds to complete a query and accuracy of the query. Each group of users after a short training session of equal times in using QBI and QBD* were given six queries of different levels of complexity in natural language. Users were given these queries in different orders in order to minimize the learning effect. In general, unskilled users did better with QBI whereas skilled ones felt more comfortable using QBD*, particularly in expressing queries characterized by a high semantic distance value involving paths of length 4, or more, and with no cycles. The reason was that skilled users perceived the whole path not as a single complex function, i.e., GA, but as a sequence of steps that can be manually built and controlled. On the other hand, there was a significant difference in accuracy and performance for queries with low semantic distance value or queries involving cycles. In the presence of cycles, QBD* users get much more confused because they see multiple copies of the same form, each corresponding to a different occurrence of the same concept (entity or relationship). On the contrary, in QBI a path corresponds to a GA and every GA is visually represented as a different icon on the screen. Therefore, when a query expression contains cycles, the user still perceives a clear distinction among different occurrences of the same concept.

When compared to the work done involving icon based visual paradigms, it is evident that a greater amount of work has been performed using form and diagrammatic paradigms. However, the small screen space of the typical notebook or palmtop computer and the limited possibility of using a keyboard, make the iconic approach particularly suitable for the users of a mobile system. In general, the main difference between QBI and the other iconic interfaces proposed in the literature [14, 29, 30] is in the way icons are defined and used for expressing concepts. In particular, other systems do not usually assign uniform semantics to icons. Also, as opposed to QBI, these systems adopt the extensional browsing approach (that is, browsing of instances in the remote database) as the principal querying strategy [27, 29] hence making them unsuitable for mobile environments that are characterized by low communication bandwidth over expensive wireless communication links.

All visual query interfaces discussed above have been proposed in the context of work-stations with large screens, graphics capabilities and pointing devices. The need for an alternative visual query paradigm for mobile, pen-based computers that takes into consideration the requirements of mobile users, such as exploration of a large database schema, and the limitations of mobile computers, such as small screen and no keyboard, was first identified in [3]. As opposed to QBI, the proposed alternative is form-based whereas the external data model is a multi-level semantic data model which uses the universal relation approach at different levels to coalesce related information and eliminate low-level information not relevant to the user. As stated earlier, the concept of GAs in QBI serves a similar purpose, coalescing related information of an object from the perspective of the user and representing it on the screen with an icon.

Recognizing that query languages which require fully specified paths are too restrictive, a number of authors have proposed various solutions. In [18], *path expressions* are examined and form the basis of the XSQL system. XSQL allows the specification of *path variables* by means of which incomplete path expressions can be specified. In [17], path expressions are considered to be abbreviated queries within a user interface to a database system. Given an ambiguous path expression which could result in multiple possible paths, the task is to find those completions most likely intended by the user.

The idea of the Universal Relation Model [22, 23, 31] is that access paths are embedded in attribute names and for every set of attributes X there is a unique basic relation that the user has in mind. This relation is computed through the *Window Function* on the set of attribute names X. Within a Window Function a *decision problem* concerning which is the most meaningful attribute is tackled. The choice of assigning a meaning to an attribute name is based on the analysis of the schema of the underlying database and various kinds of dependencies. With this approach, the same attribute name can have different meanings if used in different contexts; as a consequence, even if the user is not required to know the internal schema of the database, she/he must be aware of the domain of interest.

The idea of presenting to the user a simplified structure of the database by evaluating the semantics of the attributes, is common to both QBI and the Universal Relation approach. However, the querying strategy, is slightly different. Instead of assigning a meaning to an attribute *after* the query has been specified, QBI uses the semantic distance function to present to the user all the meaningful attributes *before* the query is composed. Moreover, the use of a semantic model and statistical information on the database extension allows the definition of a richer notion of meaningfulness of an attribute.

8. Conclusions

In this paper, we have described an icon-based query processing facility called QBI, suitable for mobile users. That is, QBI satisfies all three of the criteria identified in the introduction for an effective mobile query processing facility:

(1) QBI allows the construction of a database query with no special knowledge of how the database is structured and where it is located. Its iconic visual query language does not involve path specification in composing a query. Thus, it is equally useful to both unsophisticated and expert mobile users.
(2) Users primarily interact with the system with a pointing device, such as a pen or a mouse, and compose a query by arranging icons. Thus, it overcomes any size limitations of a mobile computer while new requirements are not imposed.
(3) QBI's algorithms, particularly the metaquery tools and GA evaluator, are designed to effectively operate under limited memory and disk capacity, limited battery power, and restricted wireless communication bandwidth.

As mentioned above, we are looking into integrated path computations under resource constraints suitable for mobile query processing. Further, we are interested in extending aspects of this work in order to minimize the amount of retrieved and transmitted data over wireless links.

Acknowledgments

This work was supported in part by National Science Foundation under grants IRI-9210588 and IRI-95020091 (USA), Integra Sistemi Interattivi, and Computer and Microimage S.p.A. (Italy). We thank S. Pavani and L. Saladini for their participation in the development of the prototype.

References

1. S. Abiteboul and A. Bonner, "Objects and views," Proceedings of the Int'l Conference ACM-SIGMOD, Denver, Colorado, June 1991, pp. 238–247.
2. R. Agrawal, S. Dar, and H. Jagadish, "Direct transitive closure algorithms: Design and performance evaluation," ACM Transaction on Database Systems, vol. 15, no. 3, 1990, pp. 427–458.
3. R. Alonso, E. Haber, and H. Korth, "A database interface for mobile computers," Proceedings of the 1992 Globecom Workshop on Networking of Personal Communication Applications, Dec. 1992.
4. R. Alonso and H. Korth, "Database issues in nomadic computing," Proceedings of ACM SIGMOD Int'l Conference on Management of Data, May 1993, pp. 388–392.
5. M. Angelaccio, T. Catarci, and G. Santucci, "QBD*: A graphical query language with recursion," IEEE Transactions on Software Engineering, vol. 16, no. 10, 1990, pp. 1150–1163.
6. A.N. Badre, T. Catarci, A. Massari, and G. Santucci, "Comparative effectiveness of a diagrammatic vs. an iconic query language," (submitted for publication), Feb. 1995.
7. C. Batini, T. Catarci, M.F. Costabile, and S. Levialdi, "Visual query systems," Technical Report No. 04.91. Dipartimento di Informatica e Sistemistica, Universita' di Roma "La Sapienza", Mar. 1991.
8. G. Bono and P. Ficorilli, "Natural language restatement of queries expressed in a graphical language," Proceedings of the 11th Int'l Conference on Entity-Relationship Approach, Germany, Oct. 1992, pp. 357–374.
9. T. Catarci and G. Santucci, "Fundamental graphical primitives for visual qery languages," Information Systems, vol. 3, no. 18, 1993, pp. 75–98.
10. P.P. Chen, "The entity relationship model toward a unified view of data," ACM Transactions on Database Systems, vol. 1, no. 1, 1976.
11. I.F. Cruz, A.O. Mendelzon, and P.T. Wood, "G+: Recursive queries without recursion," Proceedings of the 2nd Int'l Conference on Expert Database Systems, 1988, pp. 355–368.
12. R. Elmasri and G. Wiederhold, "GORDAS: A formal high-level query language for the entity-relationship model," Proceedings of the 2nd Int'l Conference on Entity-Relationship Approach, Washington, D.C., 1981, pp. 49–72.
13. R.G. Gallager, Information Theory and Reliable Communication, Wiley: New York, 1968.
14. I.P. Groette and E.G. Nillson, "SICON: An icon presentation module for an E-R database," Proceedings of the 7th Int'l Conference on Entity Relationship Approach, Roma, Italy, 1988, pp. 271–289.
15. T. Imielinski and B.R. Badrinath, "Mobile wireless computing: Challenges in data management," Communication of ACM, vol. 37, no. 10, 1994, pp. 18–28.
16. Y.E. Ioannidis, R. Ramakrishnan, and L. Winger, "Transitive closure algorithms based on graph traversal," ACM Transactions on Database Systems, vol. 18, no. 3, 1993, pp. 512–576.

17. Y.E. Ioannidis and Y. Lashkari, "Incomplete path expressions and their disambiguation," Proceedings of the ACM SIGMOD Int'l Conference on Management of Data, Minneapolis, MI, May 1994, pp. 138–149.

18. M. Kifer, W. Kim, and Y. Sagiv, "Querying object oriented databases," Proceedings of the ACM SIGMOD Int'l Conference on Management of Data, May 1992, pp. 138–149.

19. H. Kim, H. Korth, and A. Silberschatz, "PICASSO: A graphical query language," Software Practice and Experience, vol. 18, no. 3, 1988, pp. 169–203.

20. W. Kim, Introduction to Object-Oriented Databases, MIT Press: Cambridge, MA, 1990.

21. R. King and S. Melville, "Ski: A semantics-knowledgeable interface," Proceedings of the 10th Int'l Conference on Very Large Data Bases, Singapore, Aug. 1984, pp. 30–33.

22. D. Maier, D. Rozenshtein, and D.S. Warren, "Window functions," Advances in Computing Research, vol. 3, 1986, pp. 213–246.

23. D. Maier and J.D. Ullman, "Maximal objects and the semantics of universal relation databases," ACM Transactions on Database Systems, vol. 1, no. 8, 1983, pp. 1–14.

24. A. Massari, "An icon based query system for radiological data," Ph.D. Thesis, Dipartimento di Informatica e Sistemistica Universita' di Roma "La Sapienza," Nov. 1995.

25. A. Massari and P.K. Chrysanthis, "Visual query of completely encapsulated objects," Proceedings of the 5th Int'l Workshop on Research Issues in Data Engineering-Distributed Object Management, Taipei, Taiwan, March 1995, pp. 18–25.

26. A. Massari, S. Pavani, and L. Saladini, "QBI: An iconic query system for inexpert users," Proceedings of the Workshop on Advanced Visual Interfaces, Bari, Italy, June 1994, pp. 240–242.

27. A. Motro, A.D. Atri, and L. Tarantino, "KIVIEW: The design of an object oriented browser," Proceedings of the 2nd Conference on Expert Database Systems, Virginia, 1988, pp. 107–131.

28. G.H. Sockut, L.M. Burns, A. Malhotra, and K.Y. Whang, "GRAQULA: A graphical query language for entity-relationship or relational databases," Research Report RC 16877, IBM T.J. Watson Research Center, Yorktown Heights, NY, March 1991.

29. Y. Tonomura and S. Abe, "Content oriented visual interfaces using video icons for visual database systems," Proceedings of the IEEE Workshop on Visual Languages, Roma, Italy, 1989, pp. 68–73.

30. K. Tsuda, M. Hirakawa, M. Tanaka, and T. Ichikawa, "Iconic browser: An iconic retrieval system for object-oriented databases," Journal of Visual Languages and Computing, vol. 1, no. 1, 1990, pp. 59–76.

31. J.D. Ullman, "The U.R. strikes back," Proceedings of the ACM Principles of Database Systems, Los Angeles, California, 1982, pp. 10–22.

32. S. Weissman, "Changing query by icons to improve querying processing for mobile users," M.S. Project, University of Pittsburgh, May 1995.

33. K.Y. Whang, A. Malhotra, G.H. Sockut, L.M. Burns, and K.S. Choi, "Two-dimensional specification of universal quantification in a graphical database query language," Transactions on Software Engineering, vol. 18, no. 3, 1991, pp. 216–224.

34. Z. Zhang and A.O. Mendelzon, "A graphical query language for entity relationship databases," An Entity-Relationship Approach to Software Engineering, C. Davis, S. Jajodia, P. Ann-Beng NG, and R.T. Yeh (Eds.), North Holland, 1983, pp. 441–448.

35. M.M. Zloof, "Query by example," Proceedings of the National Comput. Conference, 1975, pp. 431–438.

Distributed and Parallel Databases 4, 271–288 (1996)
© 1996 Kluwer Academic Publishers.

A Mobility-Aware Dynamic Database Caching Scheme for Wireless Mobile Computing and Communications

GEORGE Y. LIU   eraliu@era-t.ericsson.se
System Research Department, Ericsson Radio Systems, S-164 80 Stockholm, Sweden

GERALD Q. MAGUIRE, JR.   maguire@it.kth.se
Department of Teleinformatics, Royal Institute of Technology, S-164 40 Stockholm, Sweden

Received May 2, 1995; Accepted February 16, 1996

Recommended by: Daniel Barbara, Ravi Jain and Narayanan Krishnakumar

Abstract. This paper describes a mobility-aware dynamic database caching scheme for wireless mobile computing and communications. A *mobile-floating agent* scheme is proposed, in which caching techniques are cognizant of the mobile nature of mobile users and the location-sensitive nature of mobile systems. The *mobile-floating agent* maintains a second class cache in the fixed network and employs Barbara's *"invalidation reports broadcasting"* cache consistency strategies to maintain a dynamic cache consistent with the first class cache in the mobile client. The *"invalidation reports broadcasting"* scheme is combined with knowledge of the mobility behavior of each individual mobile user and broadcasts of *invalidation reports* only occur within the user's mobility area. The evaluation results show that, for a large system (200 cells), this scheme can reduce the system cost by more than 87%, for even highly mobile users, compared with a fully replicated database system.

Keywords: wireless mobile computing, dynamic data caching, allocation for mobile databases, Novel applications

1. Introduction

Continuous advances in digital mobile communication technology coupled with the recent proliferation of portable computers have led development efforts for future mobile systems towards mobile computing—a new dimension for future communication and computing networks. Mobility of computers introduces challenging new problems that were not encountered in the design and implementation of either conventional mobile or fixed computer networks. In a wireless mobile environment, because the transmission is wireless, the radio[1] signals face problems of path loss, fading, interference and time dispersion. These impairments may cause higher error rates, signal disconnection, and increased communication latency resulting from re-transmissions, error-control processing, etc. Thus, wireless links often have both higher communication latency and more limited bandwidth than wired links. To hide this greater latency and more limited bandwidth (while exploiting the bursty nature of data communication) we might utilize both caching (for re-use) and prefetching of data. Caching and prefetching are *essential latency reduction techniques* and are frequently used in fixed distributed systems to reduce network traffic and server utilization [13]. How to adapt caching and prefetching in a wireless mobile environment to support mobile computing and wireless database querying, and how to efficiently integrate these techniques recognizing and accommodating the mobile nature of mobile users are the questions which we address in this paper.

Cache management issues include cache consistency polices, cache replacement and writing polices, and algorithms for cache consistency. The conventional cache management techniques, which are mainly designed for fixed networks, are inefficient in the radio environment where the communication channels are unpredictable and highly variable with time and location. In a wireless environment, mobile computers have more constraints, such as limited bandwidth, greater probability of disconnections, limited electrical power, etc., than fixed computers. In addition, the connectivity and configuration of wireless networks is highly dynamic. It may change as mobile terminals change location or as the environment around them changes. The communication bandwidth is frequently location-dependent. As a computer moves, its computing environment changes. This computing environment includes the available communication bandwidth, protocol and service availability, etc., for the mobile's current (and future) location. For example, an indoor infrared (IR) link might be several Mb/s; while Mobitex or GSM can provide an 8 kb/s link for wide area coverage. However, a cache and prefetch management system, with its associated consistency or invalidation strategy, designed for a indoor multi-Mb/s communication link is unlikely to work well for a wide area 8 kb/s link. Conversely, a system optimized for wide area 8 kbit/s links is unlikely to be satisfactory for use over the multi-Mb/s indoor link. Therefore, in order to efficiently support mobility, we argue that cache management should be aware of location and mobility.

Previous research work includes the Coda file system [11], which relies on a dynamic caching mechanism to provide disconnected operation for portable computers. Carl Tait [21] proposed a variable-consistency replication and a working-set file prefetching method to balance the consistency and availability of data for low bandwidth wireless connections. This method uses a "lazy" or "write-back" scheme in which the client simply leaves updates in its caches and servers periodically pick up these updates and propagate them to (multiple) replication sites. However, none of these earlier method are efficient for wireless links, because they use conventional cache consistency polices across low bandwidth radio links. Furthermore, they do not adequately consider the other special characteristics of the mobile wireless scenario, such as mobility, location-sensitive information, location-awareness, etc.

Barbara et al. [2, 3] have proposed very good caching strategies for mobile environments. Instead of the server sending invalidation messages to its clients or the clients querying the server to verify the validity of their caches (as in conventional cache consistency policies), Barbara's caching strategies use the broadcasting nature of wireless links to allow the server to periodically or asynchronously broadcasting *invalidation reports* which include only the items which have been updated. This scheme (which we will refer to it as *"invalidation reports broadcasting"*) can greatly reduce the uplink querying costs, while exploiting the generally greater power resources of the infrastructure and the frequently asymmetric link (with greater outgoing bandwidth) from the infrastructure to the mobile clients. However, the broadcaster should be aware of the user's mobility and probable location (mobility area). A broadcast of *invalidation reports* to a location where the user is not there, is a waste of bandwidth. For a large system which may consist of thousands of cells, it may be impractical or even impossible to have the database fully replicated at each cell or to broadcast all the *invalidation reports* within each cell. Therefore, we would like to combine the *"invalidation reports broadcasting"* scheme with knowledge of the mobility behavior of mobile users. This can be used to limit the broadcast traffic to the area where the relevant user (most likely) is.

In this paper, we propose a mobile-floating agent scheme which integrates caching techniques with cognizance of the mobile nature of mobile users and the location-sensitive nature of mobile systems. Thus, the caching strategies are aware of and dynamically accommodate the mobility of mobile users. The mobile-floating agent maintains a second class cache in the fixed network and employs Barbara's *"invalidation reports broadcasting"* caching consistency strategies to maintain a dynamic cache consistency with the first class cache in the mobile client. The *"invalidation reports broadcasting"* scheme is combined with the mobility behavior of each individual mobile user and broadcasts the *invalidation reports* only to the user's location (mobility) area. The rest of this paper is organized as followings: in Section 2, we propose a mobile floating agent scheme, Section 3 presents a mobility-aware dynamic caching scheme which combines the mobile floating agent scheme with cache consistency strategies to make the caching scheme aware of users mobility, and finally, Section 4 concerns performance evaluation.

2. Mobile-floating agent scheme

2.1. A mobile computing system architecture

Wireless mobile computing [4] refers to computing systems that provide the ability to compute and communicate within their networked environment via wireless links. This could involve mobile computing terminals/workstations/PDAs/... participating in a wireless LAN or connecting to wired networks through wireless networks or mobile networks, as shown in figure 1.

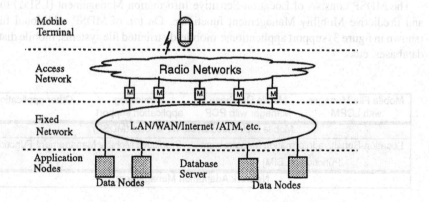

Figure 1. Wireless mobile computing systems.

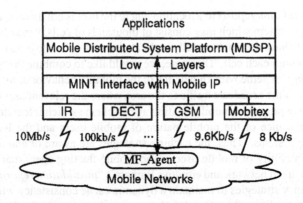

Figure 2. An MDSP platform with mobile floating agent supports mobile applications.

The wireless infrastructure of today consists of heterogeneous networks based on different standards, bandwidths, and services. It includes cellular networks, personal communications networks (PCNs), wireless LANs, point-to-point wireless links, etc. These systems span a wide range of bandwidths, ranging from ~10 kb/s, as is common in outdoor macrocells, up to 2–10 Mb/s for indoor picocells [5].

To cope with the varying bandwidth and connectivity of different links at different locations and to efficiently support service and resource mobility, we proposed [16] a Mobile Distributed System Platform (MDSP) with Mobile-Floating Agents. Figure 2 shows the relationship of the MDSP and applications in a mobile multi-link environment, i.e., several different co-existing networks, e.g., a Mobitex 8 kb/s link for a wide coverage area, an indoor infrared (IR) link, etc.

At the lower layers, the MINT (Mobile INTernet router) [5] provides different hardware interfaces. The Mobile IP [4, 9, 20] protocol is used to support host mobility. At the higher layers, the MINT software provides a common mobile distributed platform with MF-agents supporting mobile applications.

The MDSP consists of Location-Sensitive Information Management (LSIM) functions and Predictive Mobility Management functions. On top of MDSP, additional functions (shown in figure 3) support applications: mobile-distributed file systems, mobile distributed databases, etc.

Mobile File Manager with LCPM	Mobile Database Manager with PCP	Windowing application support	Other applications
Mobile Distributed System Platform (MDSP)			
Location-Sensitive Information Management Functions (LSIM)		Predictive Mobility Management Functions	
Network Adaptation Management			

Figure 3. An example of an MDSP model. LCPM: Location-dependent caching and prefetching management. PCP: Page-answer caching and prefetching functions.

The LSIM in the MDSP manages location-sensitive information and maps it to the services offered by the mobile infrastructure at specific geographical locations. It is also responsible for informing both the applications and their supporting agents of location changes and providing dynamical service connections.

The Predictive Mobility Management functions consist of: Location Prediction Functions and Floating Agent Assignment functions. The later assigns the floating agent to different locations according to the location prediction and provides service pre-connection and service/resource mobility. Location prediction can be performed automatically, by a mobile motion prediction algorithm [15], or manually, for example via a user's personal schedule.

The LSIM functions and the Mobile File System Manager with Location-dependent Caching and Prefetching Management as well as the Location Prediction Functions have been described in our previous papers [12, 16]. Thus, this paper will focus on the Mobile Floating Agent Assignment functions and the Mobile Database Management.

2.2. Mobile floating agent concepts

To distribute network services and data closer to mobile users, that is, to provide service and data mobility in wireless data networks, we propose a Mobile Floating Agent (MF-Agent) scheme. An MF-Agent is a process or a set of processes, executing on remote mobile support routers[2], that communicate with and connect to the local host resources and manage a variable replicated second class data cache on behalf of a mobile user.

An MF-agent has the following properties:

1. It is time dependent. The lifetime of an MF-agent depends on the following criteria:

   - *Timer parameter* (t_{mf}): Each MF-agent maintains a timer which is set when the MF-agent is assigned. This timer is re-set when the MF-agent is an Acting Mobile-agent (AM-agent), i.e., actively providing service.
   - *LRU parameter* (l_{mf}): Each MF-agent maintains a Least Recently Used (LRU) parameter which is updated based on MF-agent activity (actually their inactivity). The LRU parameter provides a priority index for shared resources (e.g., space for secondary cache, memory, etc.) with other MF-agents on the same node. If resources have to be reclaimed, the MF-agent(s) with the highest LRU parameter is (are) chosen as a victim(s).

2. It maintains a second class cache and dynamic cache consistency with its client.
3. It maintains an user profile for its client.

With the support of the MF-Agent, data and resources are decoupled from the underlying network and move around following their associated mobile users. Furthermore, by using the predictive mobility management functions, the service logic and user data can be pre-assigned and pre-connected at the location to which the user is moving, as shown in figure 4. (It is beyond the scope of this paper to describe the detailed mobile floating agent protocol, for details, the reader is referred to [14].)

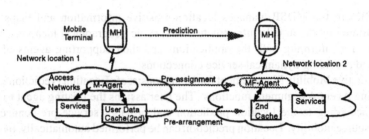

Figure 4. M-agent and MF-agent support service pre-connection and resource pre-arrangement.

2.3. *Mobile floating agent assignment algorithms*

Consider an area covered by cells with each cell serviced by a mobile support router (MSR). An MF-agent can be implemented as a software entity which consists of a set of processes, executing on remote fixed hosts or an MSR. We define m, the mobility factor during interval τ_m, i.e., m is defined as the average number of new MSRs which have been passed during time τ_m. The service rate, s, is defined as the number of MF-agents that service each unit movement of the mobile users, that is:

$$ s = \frac{d}{h \cdot m \cdot \tau_m} \tag{1} $$

where d is the service distance, h is a hierarchic factor defined as the total number of MSRs under control of each MF-agent, τ_m is a period of time during which m is sampled. The service distance represents the distance (in numbers of MSRs, i.e., cells) that a mobile can move while still being serviced by an MF-agent over the interval τ_m.

To ensure that there is at least one MF-agent supporting each user whenever the user moves, the service rate should be $s \geq 1$, that is, $d \geq hm\tau_m$. The MF-agent assignment algorithm[3] (without any movement prediction [15]) is:

1. Calculate the mobility factor m during each τ_m;
2. Define a circle centered at the current location with a radius $d = \mathrm{int}(h \cdot m \cdot \tau_m)$ and assign Mobile Floating Agents (MFAs) within the circle;
3. If at the boundary of the circle, repeat from step 1.

The result is that a mobile will be within the service area of these Mobile Floating Agents for the interval τ_m. This area defines the **probable** location of the mobile terminal. We refer to this area as the user's mobility area.

3. Mobility-aware dynamic caching and prefetching scheme

In this section, we present a hierarchic Mobility-Aware Dynamic (MAD) cache management scheme and algorithm for wireless mobile computing. The following subsections describe

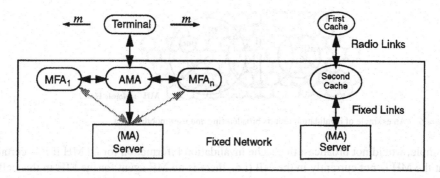

Figure 5. MAD hierarchic caches. MA: Mobility agent; AMA: Acting mobility agent; MFA: Mobile-floating agent.

the basic principles of the hierarchic MAD caching, Dynamical Caching Consistency and Mobility-aware Caching Management.

3.1. Hierarchical MAD caching consistency

The MAD Caching Scheme is designed in a hierarchy with two classes of caches: the first class is implemented in the terminal and the second class is managed by the mobile-floating agent in the network(s), as shown in figure 5.

Two classes of cache consistency schemes are deployed. First, in the fixed network, a dynamic cache consistency (DCC) algorithm (see next subsection) is used to maintain data consistency between the server and the MFAs, including the AMA. Second, between the first class cache and the second class cache, a mobility-aware cache coherence scheme is proposed in which the MF-agent keeps track of the items cached by its client and is responsible for broadcasting the invalidation report if the item is changed. Barbara's *"invalidation reports broadcasting"* cache consistency strategies [2, 3] are used to maintain dynamic cache consistency with the first class cache in the mobile client. The *"invalidation reports broadcasting"* scheme is combined with the mobility behavior of each individual mobile user and the *invalidation reports* are only broadcast to the user's probable location (mobility) area. Because the MF-agent assignment algorithm guarantees that the mobile host (MH) will be in the MF-agent's covered area, the MH will receive the *invalidation reports* if it is not disconnected or failed. The MF-agents can maintain a user profile for its client in which the disconnection behavior information ("sleepers" or "workaholics" [2, 3]) of the client is recorded. This information is sent to the MF-agents by the MH when the MF-agents are assigned. The MF-agents can change their broadcasting strategies according to the user mobility and working behavior from time to time.

The use of MF-agents has several major advantages: First, The *invalidation reports* are only broadcast to the probable location area where the MH is located. This probable location-area is dynamically changed according to the mobility behavior factor (m) of each individual MH from time to time (we call it a *dynamic location area*). A cell's MSR, for

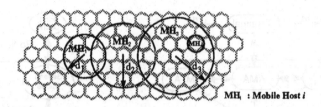

Figure 6.   An example of invalidation reports broadcasting and user mobility area.

example, would not broadcast the cache invalidation information for an MH if it is certain that the MH is not currently in the cell (i.e., there is no MF-agent for the MH in this cell). Thus, the total number (length) of *invalidation reports* broadcasted at each cell can be reduced. Figure 6 shows an example (snapshot) of invalidation reports broadcast areas for different mobile hosts (MH), each of which may have a different mobility factor. These areas may overlap, change over time and move when the mobile users change mobility behavior (during each time period τ_m).

Second, the database is only replicated at the cell or station within each user's *dynamic location area*. This can reduce the update overhead for low mobility users since their *dynamic location areas* will be small. One can think of this as an information radius, which decreases as the certainty of the user's location increases.

Third, with the support of the MF-agents in the fixed network, individualized dynamic invalidation reports can be defined for each MH according to its mobility behavior or cache consistency required during each time period τ_m.

Furthermore, with the support of the MF-agents, we have created a "virtual fully replicated database" at each cell (or MSR) for each individual MH. The database is dynamically replicated in the neighborhood of the user's probable location and changes according to the user's mobility behavior. With the predictive mobility management algorithm's support [15], whenever a user moves to another location, the user will always find the data s/he needed replicated at current cell or location. We call this an "individual virtual fully replicated database".

The caches in the MF-agents can be constructed so that they perform the same functions as a Page-answer Database [10], which is derived from the server database. Each time a query is issued by its MH, it is first evaluated in the second cache in the MF-agent, then any remaining tuples are obtained from the server database. For example, consider a set of n named data items which consists of the Page-Answers $D_i = \{p_{i_1}, p_{i_2}, \ldots, p_{i_n}\}$ with $D_{i_1} = \{p_{i_1}, p_{i_2}, \ldots, p_{i_{n-1}}\}$ prestored in the second cache. A query $q_1 = \{\langle p_{i_1} - q_{i_1}\rangle, \langle p_{i_2} - q_{i_2}\rangle, \ldots, \langle p_{i_n} - q_{i_n}\rangle\}$ can be fully reconstructed by evaluating of p_{i_n} from the server database and D_{i_1} from the second cache. A similar construction is used for the first class cache at the MH.

3.2.   Dynamical caching consistency

In the fixed network, the Dynamical Cache Consistency (DCC) scheme dynamically maintains two types of cache consistencies. Between the M-Agent (MA) and the Acting M-Agent

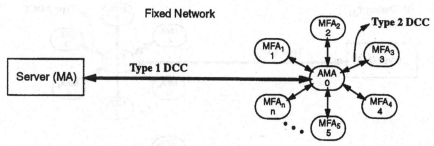

Figure 7. An example of the dynamical caching consistency.

(AMA) or the Transition M-Agent (TMA), the first type of dynamic cache consistency is maintained; and the second type of DCC is used between the AMA and its MFAs, as shown in figure 7. The structure of the MFAs shown in figure 7 is just an example. The MFAs can be distributed in different patterns depending on the MFA assignment algorithm used [15].

The type 1 DCC uses a "call-back" consistency policy. The M-Agent is responsible for keeping track of the cache status information of its AMA or TMA. To avoid frequent changes in the association with different agents as the terminal moves back and forth, the TMA is used as a temporary transit agent to forward the type 1 DCC information to the current AMA. The association between an M-Agent and an AMA will last a period of time τ_{d1}, even when the AMA becomes a TMA, i.e., the mobile terminal has moved to another location. The interval τ_{d1} is given by

$$\tau_{d1} = \frac{h\alpha_{d1}}{m} \tag{2}$$

where α_{d1} is a delay factor, h is a hierarchy factor and m is the mobility of a user during time period τ_m.

The new AMA is responsible for informing the M-Agent to establish the type 1 DCC association with it after the time period τ_{d1}. Since the M-Agent is only allowed to have type 1 DCC association with one of the MF-agents associated with each mobile user, all the other type 1 DCC associations with the old TMAs will be canceled after the association is formed with the new AMA. For example, if the mobile terminal has moved from its location 0, i.e., the current AMA, to location 1, as shown in figure 8. Then, MFA$_1$ becomes the new AMA and the previous AMA at location 0 becomes a TMA. The association between the M-Agent (MA) and the agent at the location 0, i.e., the TMA, will not be changed during the time period τ_{d1}. Instead, the TMA is responsible for transmitting type 1 DCC information to and from the current AMA. After τ_{d1}, the new AMA informs the M-Agent (MA) to establish an association with the M-Agent and, at the same time, the M-Agent (MA) removes the old one.

The type 2 DCC uses a delayed "write-update" consistency policy. The AMA and TMA will multicast or group-cast (group broadcast) the latest update to its MFA group (i.e., those in the dynamic location area) after a time interval τ_{d2}. The interval τ_{d2} is given by

$$\tau_{d2} = \frac{h\alpha_{d2}}{m} \tag{3}$$

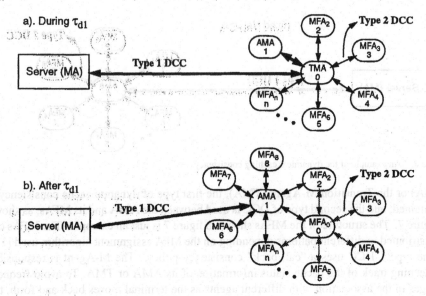

Figure 8. An example of transitions before and after τ_d.

where $\alpha_{d2}(\alpha_{d2} \geq 1)$ is a delay factor, h is a hierarchy factor and m is the mobility of a user during time period τ_m. The reason for delay τ_{d2} is that there is no need to update the caches in MFAs other than that of the AMA before $\frac{1}{m}$, i.e., the time needed for a mobile user with mobility m to move from one cell to another. During the interval τ_{d2} there may be several updates performed at the AMA; however, only the latest update is group-cast to the MFAs in the group.

For a LAN based infrastructure network architecture, a "snooping" consistency policy can be used. Each MFA in the group snoops the traffic on the LAN (if all the MFAs in the group are on the same LAN) between the M-Agent and their AMA and updates its cache. In this case, the traffic cost on the LAN to maintain a group of N MFAs is the same as that of the single AMA, i.e., no extra network traffic is generated.

4. Performance evaluations

In this section we shall analyze and evaluate the performance of our mobility-aware dynamic caching and prefetching scheme.

4.1. System model

The MF-agent architecture discussed in the previous section can be summarized in the following MF-agent model, as shown in figure 9A.

The links in the fixed network are assumed to have higher bandwidth than the wireless links. The link between an MA and an AMA may consist of multiple switches, routers, and nodes. We further assume that the longer the link, the more switches, routers and nodes may be encountered along the link, and thus, the greater the latency will be. Let D be the

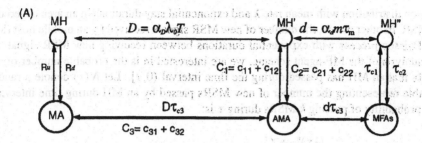

Figure 9. The MF-agent model.

logical distance, in terms of numbers of cells, between an MA and an AMA. Thus, D is a function of the mobility λ_0 (described below) and is given by

$$D = \alpha_D h \lambda_0 T \tag{4}$$

where α_D is a factor[4], $\frac{1}{2\pi} \leq \alpha_D \leq 1$, and T is the time a user moves from his home network to the MSR where the AMA is activated.

Similarly, d, the distance between an AMA and an MFA is given by

$$d = \alpha_d h m \tau_m \tag{5}$$

where α_d is a factor, $\frac{1}{2\pi} \leq \alpha_d \leq 1$, m is defined as the average number of new MSRs which have been passed during time τ_m.

Let C_1 denote the uplink cost of sending a cache consistency check message from a mobile host (MH) to its MA (or AMA), and let C_2 denote the cost of broadcasting an *invalidation report* using the down link. Let C_3 denote the cost of sending a message between an MA and its MFA per unit of movement. C_1, C_2 and C_3 can be subdivided into on-line costs: c_{11}, c_{21} and c_{31}; on-line delay (from the user's point of view): τ_{c1}, τ_{c2} and τ_{c3}, and background costs (increased background system load): c_{12}, c_{22} and c_{32}. The cost matrix is shown in figure 9B. The values of these cost parameters depend on the underlying network architecture.

4.2. Assumptions

To analyze the performance of the MF-agent scheme without loss of generality, we assume the number of MSRs a user has passed during a time interval $(0, t]$, i.e., $T = (0, t]$, is

Poisson distribution with mean rate λ and exponential stay durations in an area covered by an MSR. In other words, the number of new MSR signals received by an mobile host (MH) is a Poisson process with exponential durations between receiving new MSR signals. In our analysis of the MF-agent scheme, we are interested in is the probable number of new MSRs that an MH has passed during the time interval $(0, t]$. Let $N(\tau)$ denote a random variable representing the number of new MSRs passed by an MH during time interval τ. The probability of passing k MSRs during τ is:

$$P[N(\tau) = k] = \frac{(\lambda\tau)^k \cdot e^{-\lambda\tau}}{k!} \quad \text{where } k = 0, 1, 2, \ldots. \tag{6}$$

Thus, the probability of passing more than k (including k) MSRs during τ is:

$$P[N(\tau) \geq k] = \sum_{i=k}^{\infty} \left(\frac{(\lambda\tau)^i \cdot e^{-\lambda\tau}}{i!} \right) \quad k = 0, 1, 2, \ldots. \tag{7}$$

Let the total number of MSRs or cells be N and assume that $N \gg (m \cdot \tau_m)$, where $m \cdot \tau_m$ is the total number of new MSRs a user with a mobility m has passed during time interval τ_m, and $\tau_m \gg \tau_{c3}$, where τ_{c3} is the time required to send a message between two MF-agents, and $\tau_m < T$. It is further assumed that the mobile user is initially within their home network, and $h = 1$.

We also assume that the updates of an item in the database have an exponential distribution with an update rate of μ per item, i.e., $P_{ud} = e^{-\mu t}$. The database server is assumed to broadcast the invalidation report every L minutes.

In carrying out the analysis, we will assumed that the up-link cost is four times as significant as the down-link cost due to power (battery) constraints of the MH. It is also assumed that the on-line costs are twice as significant as the background costs and the same as the wireless and wired ones. Today, the cost of a wireless link is about 20 time higher than that of a wired link. The higher this rate is, the less significant the MF-agent assignment overhead. We believe this rate will go down to ~ 2 in the future, thus making the assignment overhead more significant; therefore we have made this worst case assumption in the analysis below. The "on-line costs" consist of the cost of a system performing a data access for a user and the cost of the user waiting for the data, i.e., the query delay costs from the user's point of view. While the background costs consists only of the cost of send the data.

4.3. Costs analysis

In this subsection we analyze and compare the costs of a system with the MF-agent scheme to that of a fully replicated system.

For a system with the support of MF-agents, as stated earlier, the number of new cells a user has passed during a time interval $(0, t] = T$ is assumed to have Poisson distribution and the duration of a stay in a cell is exponentially distributed. Let λ be the average movement

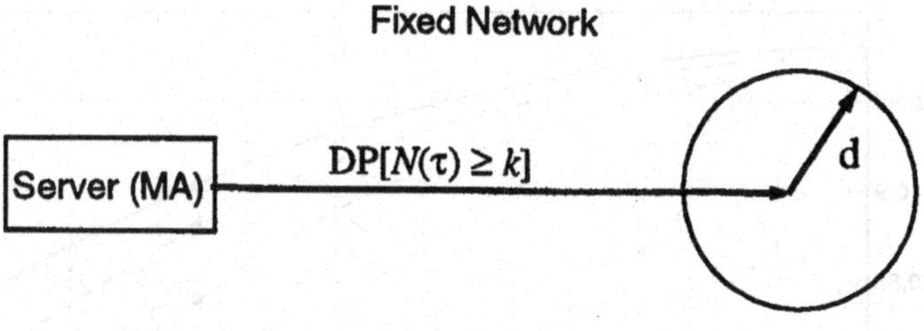

Fixed Network

Figure 10. An example of the MF-agents with radius-d assignment pattern.

rate during T. The probability of passing more than λT cells (including λT) during the period T is

$$P[N(T) \geq \lambda T] = \sum_{k=\lambda T}^{\infty} \left(\frac{(\lambda T)^k e^{-\lambda T}}{k!} \right) \quad T \geq 0, (0 \leq \lambda \leq 1) \tag{8}$$

So, the cost of the wired network to maintain the second cache consistency for a mobile user with the average movement or mobility rate λ is:

$$k_{\text{wired}} = D \cdot P[N(T) \geq \lambda T]C_3 = \alpha_D \lambda T P[N(T) \geq \lambda T] \cdot C_3 \tag{9}$$

The cost of broadcasting invalidation reports at each cell within the radius d (as shown in figure 10) every L minutes during T is:

$$K_{\text{bc}} = \pi d^2 \cdot \frac{T}{L} C_2 = \frac{\pi T}{L} (\alpha_d m \tau_m)^2 C_2 \tag{10}$$

The MF-agents have to be re-assigned when the MH is moved at the boundary of the circle. The cost of the assignment during the time interval $(0, t] = T$ is:

$$K_{\text{assig}} = \frac{T}{\tau_m} C_1 \tag{11}$$

Thus, adding Eqs. (8)–(11), the total cost of the MF-agent scheme is a function of average movement rate λ and the mobility m during τ_m is:

$$K_{\text{MF}} = \frac{T}{\tau_m} C_1 + \frac{\pi T}{L} (\alpha_d m \tau_m)^2 C_2 + \alpha_D \lambda T \sum_{k=\lambda T}^{\infty} \left(\frac{(\lambda T)^k e^{-\lambda T}}{k!} \right) \cdot C_3 \tag{12}$$

For a fully replicated system with a total of N cells, the cost of sending invalidation reports every L minutes during T (including the update and consistency of the N cells) is:

$$K_N = NC_3 + \frac{T}{L} NC_2 \tag{13}$$

$$\tag{14}$$

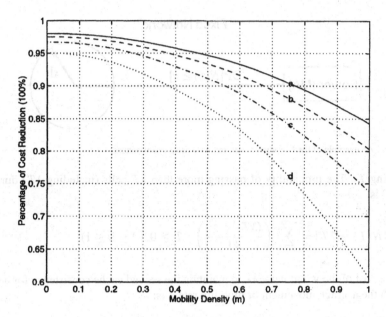

Figure 11. The percentage of cost reduction vs. the mobility m. Curve: a) $N = 500$, b) $N = 400$, c) $N = 300$, d) $N = 200$.

If, as stated above, we assume $C_1 = 4C_2$ and $C_2 = 2C_3$, then the percentage of cost reduction by using the MF-agent is:

$$
G = \frac{K_N - K_{\text{MF}}}{K_N}
$$

$$
= \frac{N\left(1 + \frac{2T}{L}\right) - \left(\frac{8T}{\tau_m} + \frac{2\pi T}{L}(\alpha_d m \tau_m)^2 + \alpha_D \lambda T \sum_{k=\lambda T}^{\infty} \left(\frac{(\lambda T)^k e^{-\lambda T}}{k!}\right)\right)}{N\left(1 + \frac{2T}{L}\right)}
\tag{15}
$$

where $\frac{1}{2\pi} \leq \alpha_D \leq 1$ and $\frac{1}{2\pi} \leq \alpha_d \leq 1$.

The percentage of cost reduction (G) versus the mobility (m) is shown in figure 11. It is assumed that $T = 100$ minutes, $\alpha_D = \alpha_d = 0.975$, average movement rate $\lambda = 0.5$, $\tau_m = 10$ minutes and $L = 10$ minutes.

It can be seen that the MF-agent scheme cuts the costs of the cache consistency operations in a system with more than 200 cells by more than 60% for any degree of mobility. For a large system with $N = 500$ cells, this scheme can reduce the cost by more than 80% for any mobility. Therefore, the MF-agent scheme is most suitable for large mobile systems with high user mobility.

The percentage of cost reduction with different broadcast intervals L is shown in figure 12 with the assumption of $T = 100$ minutes, $N = 500$, $\alpha_D = \alpha_d = 0.975$, average movement rate $\lambda = 0.5$, $\tau_m = 10$ minutes. As shown in figure 12, the longer the broadcasting interval L is, the lower the cost reduction. This is because a large broadcasting interval L also

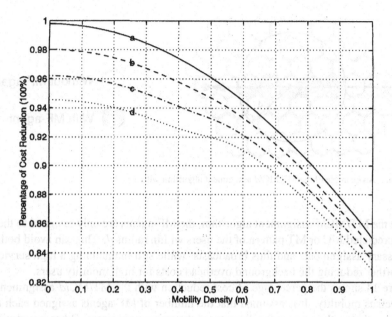

Figure 12. The percentage of cost reduction vs. the mobility m. Curve: a) $L = 1$ minute, b) $L = 10$ minutes, c) $L = 20$ minutes, d) $L = 30$ minutes.

reduces the cost for the N replicated system. However, increasing also reduces the degree of consistency; because an update (or an invalidation report) will wait longer before being broadcasted.

As can be seen the cost reduction decreases as the mobility increases. This is because as the mobility increases, the background network load will increase due to the increased d, resulting in fixed network load C_3 increasing. However, even for the highly mobile users, the proposed MF-agent scheme reduces the cost by more than 80%.

A better assignment algorithm is to combine the MFA assignment with the predictive mobility management [15]. The MF-agents are only assigned to the predicted Movement Track (MT) or Movement Circle (MC). As an MT or MC can cover a very long physical distance, only the states or cells in the MT or MC within the distance d are assigned each time (we call this the MT/MC/d assignment algorithm).

To state this more succinctly, the MT/MC/d assignment algorithm is as follows.

1. Calculate the mobility factor m during each τ_m;
2. Define a circle centered at the current location with a radius (assume the $\alpha_d = 1$, i.e., 100% confidence that the user is within the circle with radius d during τ_m) $d = \text{int}(hm\tau_m)$;
3. Only assign the MFAs to the MSRs located on the predicted MT or MC within the circle;
4. If at the boundary of the circle, repeat from step 1.

A comparison of the assignments made by the MT/MC/d and the radius d algorithm (for $d = 3$) is shown in figure 13.

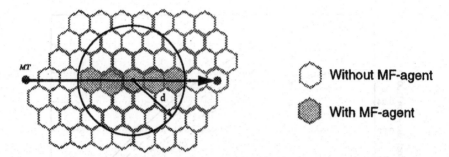

Figure 13. An example of the MT/MC/d assignment algorithm with $d = 3$.

With the MT/MC/d assignment algorithm, the MF-agents are only assigned to the states on the predicted MC or MT pattern of the users within radius d. This can avoid both many unnecessary assignments and thus broadcasts, while still maintaining a high service rate; thus, further reducing the background overhead costs for high mobility users.

Figure 14 shows the percentage of cost reduction with the MT/MC/d assignment algorithm versus mobility. It is assumed that the number of MF-agents assigned each time is $2(\alpha_d m \tau_m)$, that is, the same as the diameter of the assignment circle. Other assumptions are the same as used in figure 11. As shown in figure 14, if the prediction accuracy of the predictive mobility management function is larger than 0.9 and $N \geq 200$, then the MT/MC/d

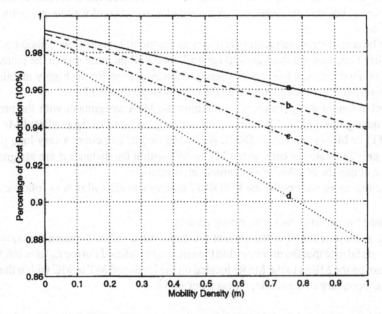

Figure 14. The percentage of cost reduction of a system using MT/MC/d rather than full replication vs. the mobility m. Curve: a) $N = 500$, b) $N = 400$, c) $N = 300$, d) $N = 200$.

assignment algorithm improves the cost reduction by almost 30% (from more than 60% in figure 11 to more than 87%) for any mobility. Even for highly mobile (but predictable) users there can be a very significant reduction in the costs of maintaining the user's cache, as compared to a fully replicated scheme.

5. Summary and conclusion

In this paper, we have proposed a mobility-aware, dynamic caching management scheme for wireless mobile computing. In order to efficiently support mobility, we have combined the cache techniques with an MF-agent scheme, which makes it possible for the caching strategies to be aware of and dynamically cope with the mobility of mobile users. The evaluation results clearly indicate the feasibility and the performance gain in terms of the system cost reduction for this new concept. It is shown that, for a large system with 200 or more cells, using the predictive MF-agent assignment algorithm can reduce the system cost by more than 87%, for even highly mobile users, compared with a fully replicated database system.

Acknowledgment

We would like to thank Prof. Björn Pehrson, Prof. Marilyn E. Noz, Dr. Alexander Marlevi, Expert Anders Danne and Prof. Jens Zander for helpful discussions, comments and their support of this work. We would also like to thank the anonymous reviewers for their valuable comments and suggestions on the manuscript.

Notes

1. For simplicity we refer to the signals as radio signals, although they might actually be Infrared, Radio, ...
2. They might also execute on mobile service servers, each of which is associated with multiple wireless access points, i.e., gateways between the wired and wireless networks.
3. For details of the predictive assignment algorithms, the reader is referred to [15] or [17].
4. The equations are given for 2-dimensional (2D) networks, a similar set exists for the 3D case.

References

1. B.R. Badrinath, A. Arup, and T. Imielinski, "Structuring distributed algorithms for mobile hosts," Technical Report, Department of Computer Science, Rutgers University, June 1993.
2. D. Barbara and T. Imielinski, "Sleepers and Workaholics: Caching strategies in mobile environments," Technical Report MITL-TR-58-93, MITL, June 1993.
3. D. Barbara and T. Imielinski, "Sleepers and Workaholics: Caching strategies in mobile environments," Mobidata, An Interactive Journal of Mobile Computing, vol. 1, no. 1, 1994.
4. D. Duchamp, S.K. Feiner, and G.Q. Maguire, Jr., "Software technology for wireless mobile computing," IEEE Network Magazine, Nov. 1991.
5. R. Hager, A. Klemets, G.Q. Maguire, Jr., M.T. Smith, and F. Reichert, "MINT—A mobile internet router," Proceedings of the IEEE Vehicular Technology Conference '93, Institute of Electrical and Electronics Engineers, May 18–20, 1993.

6. S. Hoffpauir and J. Parker, "Impact of terminal mobility on the intelligent network," The 6th International Conference on Wireless Communications, Calgary, Canada, July 11–13, 1994.

7. T. Imielinski and B.R. Badrinath, "Querying in highly mobile and distributed environments," in Proceedings of the Eighteen International Conference on Very Large Databases, Vancouver, Aug. 1992.

8. T. Imielinski and A. Acharya, "The network as a database machine," Mobidata, An Interactive Journal of Mobile Computing, vol. 1, no. 2, 1995.

9. J. Ioannidis and G.Q. Maguire, Jr., "The design and implementation of a mobile internetworking architecture," USENIX Winter 1993 Technical Conference, USENIX Association, Jan. 1993, pp. 491–502.

10. N. Kamel and R. King, "Intelligent database caching through the use of page-answers and page-traces," ACM Transactions on Database Systems, vol. 17, no. 4, 1992.

11. J.J. Kistler and M. Satyanarayanan, "Disconnected operation in the Coda file system," ACM Trans. on Computer Systems, vol. 10, no.1, 1992.

12. G. Liu, "Exploitation of location-dependent caching and prefetching techniques for supporting mobile computing and communications," The 6th International Conference on Wireless Communications, Calgary, Canada, July 11–13, 1994.

13. G. Liu and G. Q. Maguire, "A survey of caching and prefetching techniques in distributed systems," Technical Report, Royal Institute of Technology, Oct. 1994.

14. G. Liu and G.Q. Maguire, Jr., "A virtual distributed system architecture for supporting global-distributed mobile computing," Technical Report, ITR 95-01, Dec. 1994.

15. G. Liu and G. Maguire, Jr., "A predictive mobility management scheme for wireless mobile computing," Tech. Report, Royal Institute of Technology, TRITA-ITR 95-04, Feb. 1995.

16. G. Liu and G.Q. Maguire, Jr., "Efficient mobility management support for wireless data services," Proceedings of 45th IEEE Vehicular Technology Conference (VTC'95), Chicago, Illinois, July 26–28, 1995.

17. G. Liu, "Efficient mobility management for wireless mobile computing and communications," Licentiate Thesis, Royal Institute of Technology, IT-R 95:07, March 1995.

18. R. Nevoux and S. Tabbane, "Mobility features for personal and terminal UMTS communications," The 6th International Conference on Wireless Communications, Calgary, Canada, July 11–13, 1994.

19. A. Papoulius, Probability, Random Variables, and Stochastic Processes, Third Edition, McGraw-Hill International Editions, 1991.

20. C. Perkins (Ed.), "Mobility support in IP, version 15," IETF, Internet Draft, Jan. 1996.

21. C.D. Tait, "A file system for mobile computing," Ph.D. Thesis, Columbia University, 1993.

22. K.S. Trivedi, Probability & Statistics with Reliability, Queuing, and Computer Science Applications, Prentice-Hall, Inc.: Englewood Cliffs, NJ 07632.